the oracles

Praise for *The Oracles: My Filipino Grandparents in America*

Pati Navalta Poblete's *The Oracles* is a tender, funny, and engrossing memoir about the arrival of her four Filipino grandparents in America. Together they upend her American world of *Charlie's Angels*, *The Brady Bunch*, Nabisco wafers, and chocolate milk with the jazzy sound of snapping peas, fragrant spices, and sage advice. Through their unsolicited beads of wisdom they awaken an invisible thread like the precious string of a rosary, binding Pati's heart back to her homeland.
—Tess Uriza Holthe, author of *When the Elephants Dance*

The Oracles is a brave and touching book that made me laugh....Regarding the Asian American experience, there need to be more books like hers that explore the range of emotions one feels when balancing filial piety with one's desire to listen to Billy Idol.
—Kim Wong Keltner, author of *The Dim Sum of All Things* and *Buddha Baby*

This memoir is sweet without being coy, affectionate without being too sentimental, both witty and funny. It takes us into Pati's heart and reminds us to remember our grandparents' stories. They are worth telling.
—Leny Mendoza Strobel, author of *Coming Full Circle: The Process of Decolonization Among Post-1965 Filipino Americans*

I laughed and cried as Pati Navalta Poblete drew me into her wonderful, idiosyncratic Filipino American family—a kind of *Cheaper by the Dozen*, only hers was full of grandparents whose strange and mysterious ways offer universal lessons in life.
—Helen Zia, author of *Asian American Dreams: The Emergence of an American People*

With the ease and experience of a veteran writer, this youthful talent weaves her tale with all the naturalness and freshness of raindrops falling....Like her Grandpa Paterno always said: "Be good, Neneng. Make us all proud." I can see him, all four of the grandparents, as well as her parents, and her people, and her fellow Filipino American writers like me swelling with pride.
—Oscar Peñaranda, author of *Seasons by the Bay* and *Full Deck (Jokers Playing)*

the oracles

My Filipino Grandparents in America

Pati Navalta Poblete

Heyday Books, Berkeley, California

This book was made possible in part by a generous grant from the BayTree Fund.

Library of Congress Cataloging-in-Publication Data
Poblete, Pati Navalta.
  The oracles : my Filipino grandparents in America / Pati Navalta Poblete.
    p. cm.
  ISBN 978-1-59714-036-2
  1. Poblete, Pati Navalta—Childhood and youth. 2. Poblete, Pati Navalta—Family. 3. Filipino American families—California—San Francisco. 4. Filipino Americans—California—San Francisco—Biography. 5. Intergenerational relations—California—San Francisco. 6. Grandparents—California—San Francisco—Biography. 7. Immigrants—California—San Francisco—Biography. 8. Grandparents—Philippines—Biography. 9. San Francisco (Calif.)—Biography. I. Title.
  F869.S39F46 2006
  305.89'921079461—dc22
  [B]
                        2006013954

Cover photograph courtesy of the author
Book design by Rebecca LeGates
Printing and Binding: McNaughton & Gunn, Saline, MI

Orders, inquiries, and correspondence should be addressed to:
     Heyday Books
     P. O. Box 9145, Berkeley, CA 94709
     (510) 549-3564, Fax (510) 549-1889
     www.heydaybooks.com

Printed in the United States of America

10 9 8 7 6 5 4 3 2

For Robby and Julie

Contents

Preface

The steady snapping of green beans provided the rhythm that moved our household. Not incessant like the haunting drip of a leaky faucet, but inspiring like the cool clicking of fingers in a jazz club.

That's the sound I woke up to many mornings as I got out of bed and many evenings as I prepared to crawl back in.

My two grandmothers sat at the kitchen table in their floral housedresses with a heap of long Chinese green beans in front of them. I watched their swift choreographed movements—one snip at each end, then three snips breaking the long rope into four parts. They filled Ziploc bags and stacked them in the freezer.

The beat reached into the patio where it met the melody of my two whistling grandfathers. They spent hours in the backyard together, working in the vegetable garden, cleaning the fish they had just caught, or sitting with an ice-cold San Miguel dark beer.

Sometimes I took my place at the table, snapping along with the grandmothers and listening to the lyrics of their conversation. Other times I sat on the stairs where I had a view of all of them—each playing their own tune, their own instrument, but coming together to create this strange soundtrack of my everyday life.

The Oracles

"The Oracles" I called them as I grew older—my four grandparents whom my mom and dad had brought from the Philippines to watch over my brother and me. One by one they came, changing the flavors of my food, the aromas in my home, the thoughts in my mind.

But there were other days when they were far from harmonious. When the strangeness of their foreign lands surfaced in my American life and shook its foundation. That's when the snapping silenced and the movements ceased.

Those were the days I realized that as much as I sometimes longed for them to disappear, my life would never be the same without their music.

the oracles

Chapter One

The Latchkey Life

I plopped down and sank into the green vinyl beanbag in front of our wood-paneled Zenith television. The sun had already gone down, and the house was eerily still. I turned up the volume dial on the TV, like I did every day during this time, and filled the silence with the voices of the Brady Bunch family.

I imagined I was one of them—even speaking to them from time to time. "Alice told me to make my own snack today," I told my imaginary white mother, Carol, as I made my peanut butter and jelly sandwich. "Marcia, are we going to join the Girl Scouts?"

To any outsider, I may have seemed certifiably insane, but I wasn't. I was a latchkey kid.

From the moment my parents saw me off to the bus stop in the morning to the second I heard them open the garage door at night, I was on my own, and I loved it.

The rules were simple: Don't go out, don't let anyone in, don't tell anyone I'm alone, and call 911 if there was an emergency. My days were simple and carefree, and today was no different.

Every afternoon I walked three blocks from the bus stop to our house on Lexington Drive in Livermore, California. I looked carefully to make sure no one saw me opening the door with my own key before I went in. I went straight to my room to change, then headed to the backyard to play.

Yober, our Alaskan Malamute, would be waiting for me. He was a big bear of a dog and I spent hours playing fetch with him. He was my babysitter, my dad often told me.

Dad felt guilty every time he and my mom left for work. "Be a good girl," he said that morning with a look of sadness in his eyes that had become all too familiar. Mom never seemed to be that sad. She was one of eleven children in the Philippines, so she knew what it was like to fend for herself. "Don't cook anything on the stove" was her motto.

When I was hungry, I snacked on celery sticks with peanut butter, or Nabisco's Nilla Wafers with milk. Simple sandwiches and root beer floats were fine dining for me. I didn't have friends in the neighborhood to play with because I wasn't allowed to open the door. So I invented them.

When I was feeling adventurous, Sabrina and Kelly from *Charlie's Angels* were my best friends. I named myself "Heather" because it sounded pretty and blonde. Most other days, I was just "Kimberly," the lost Brady the family never noticed was Asian. I used my imagination to fill up my time, and basked in my independence. The only chores I had were to do my homework, keep my room clean, and feed the dog. Other than that, the day was my own.

But soon, I was told, Mom would be having her baby. My little brother or sister would keep me from being so lonely and everything would be grand and lovely. I wondered if that meant my little brother or sister would be left alone with me after school, but that was a fleeting thought, as most thoughts are when you're seven years old. I never bothered to ask my parents what would happen once the baby was here.

I dropped my lunch pail in our tiled entryway and ran to the bathroom. Earlier that afternoon I'd spent my extra change to get a second half-pint of chocolate milk, and it had upset my stomach for the rest of the day.

When I emerged from the bathroom, I prepared to change into my play clothes and head to the backyard to see the dog.

"Hey," I heard a voice from the family room.

I jumped and gave out a little yell. It was a school day, and I was always alone in the house. In my haste, I didn't notice that Mom was sitting in the green beanbag with my newborn brother nestled in her arms.

"This is Christopher," she said, "your brother."

I walked over and knelt on the floor next to both of them. My brother had a small knitted cap on, and his tiny hands were clenched into fists. My mom looked tired but glowing and content.

I didn't need to make my peanut butter and jelly sandwich that day. The kitchen was filled with dishes from friends and relatives—casseroles, noodles, soups, desserts. Mom told me she and my brother would be there from now on when I came home from school. Somehow, I thought she meant forever, and that made me happy.

During the next few months, I didn't miss my imaginary friends. I ran home from the bus every day, excited to see what my brother was doing. Mom always had something ready for me in the kitchen, and the house always smelled so warm and sweet when I opened the door.

Dad came home from work more often. The four of us lounged in the family room and played with the baby while watching Donny and Marie or Lawrence Welk and his bubbles. My dad also began taking days off from work to volunteer at my school. Once, he chaperoned a field trip we took to a nearby ranch, and another time he came to my class to talk about being a journalist in the Philippines.

My classmates and I sat with our legs crossed on the round carpet while my dad stood in front of the chalkboard and explained the process of getting a news story and being edited. He proudly took the old, brown-edged press badge he was issued in Manila and let everyone pass it around. Nobody understood what that press badge meant or what he was talking about, so he quickly lost their attention.

"Look," I heard one boy whisper behind me. "He's a Chinese

man. He's talking Chinese." Everyone behind me giggled. I looked at my dad, who had taken the day off so that he could come to my school and make me proud.

"You shut up!" I turned around and screamed. "We're not Chinese!"

My dad stopped talking and looked at me in shock. I began to cry, feeling sorry for both my dad and myself. I hated going to a school where I was the only minority, and I hated myself for being that minority.

Instead of praising me for defending our family's honor, I was scolded the whole way home. "Who cares what they say, as long as you know who you are," my dad said. "You have to know how to behave when you're in school. They make fun of you because you look different, but that's what makes you unique," he said.

I slumped in the passenger seat, hearing nothing but "blah, blah, blah."

"Why do I have to be Asian?" I whined. "Everybody makes fun of me."

"You listen to me," he said with a stern voice I had never heard before. "You can't change who you are or where you came from. You can try to be something else, but those kids who made fun of you will always see someone who is different. You can hate it or be proud of it."

I hated it.

Christopher was a few months old when my mom decided she wanted to go back to work. I knew she and my dad had been talking about it, but I didn't realize how quickly it would all happen. I wondered if this meant I would go back to my latchkey routine, and who would take care of the baby when I was in school.

"Someone is coming to help us so you and Chris won't have to be alone," my mom said. "It's a big surprise."

Until that surprise came, my parents strapped my brother into his car seat and into their commuter car, in between my dad's black Samsonite briefcase and my mom's overstuffed leather bag. One of my mom's friends who had sent for her parents from the Philippines to care for her own children told my mom they could handle watching my brother until we found a permanent babysitter.

I dug up my red-string necklace with its house-key amulet, resurrected my imaginary companions, and assumed the old routine.

I was eight years old when the "big surprise" finally came. Just by virtue of the word "surprise," I had expected something joyous and extraordinary. I didn't expect the surprise to be a 140-pound, five-foot-three old woman. I only found out later that she was, indeed, extraordinary, in the sense that she was nothing like anyone I knew, or cared to know. But her arrival was not joyous—not in the least bit.

My mom had sent to the Philippines for her mother, my Grandma Fausta, to take care of my brother and me while my parents worked. My father had just been promoted to Director of Corporate Planning—a title I never understood—for Blue Cross in Oakland, and my mom had just landed a full-time job as an account executive at Union Bank. "It will be better to have your grandma here with you instead of hiring a stranger," my mom said.

There wasn't much preparation. A week before she arrived, my parents casually mentioned that my grandmother would be here soon. I envisioned a Mary Poppins type, singing catchy tunes laced with life lessons. At the very least, she would be a sweet old lady, adorable like Betty White and dependable like Alice on *The Brady Bunch*.

I held my dad's hand at the airport, waiting for my fantasy grandmother to walk onto the tarmac at San Francisco International Airport. I caught a glimpse of several candidates, expecting them to tear up at the sight of me and then cover my face with powder-infused kisses. But they each latched onto other families.

Suddenly, my mom let out a little yell: *"Mang!"* The word,

which I later found out was short for *"Mamang,"* was foreign to me.

I looked up and saw a short, stout woman with pursed lips and shrewd eyes. Her bosoms sagged to her bulging belly, and her thin nylons couldn't conceal the varicose veins beneath them.

"This is Grandma," my mom said, nudging me toward her. I looked up and stared as she waited for me to take her hand to my forehead—a sign of respect in Filipino culture.

But the look in her eyes made me nervous.

She wasn't Mary, Betty, or Alice. She was a woman who had raised eleven kids in the Philippines and had already helped raise dozens of other grandchildren. Now she was in America to raise even more. She was an immigrant who came not for her own American Dream but that of her daughter.

And she was only the first of four strangers who were about to turn my life upside down.

. . .

I was born in the Philippine island of Ilocos Norte on August 15, 1916. I am the oldest of three children. My sister, Leunarda, is three years younger than me. I do not like her so much. My brother, Maximo, was the youngest and died very young. I do not want to talk about him.

I met your Grandpa Domingo after our family moved to the province of Kiamba on the Philippine island of Mindanao. He came to work on my uncle's farm.

Oh, I had many suitors before I met him, all very handsome, and some rich. Maybe it is because I always dressed so nice. I always fixed myself as if I was going to a party. My nails were always painted and manicured. I chose your grandpa because he was the kindest and most hardworking.

When he began courting me, my mother and father were very angry. He was just a poor worker, they said. My sister told me that he would never become anything. But we still married. She was like sure.

Nothing? How could she say he was nothing? Never mind. After we married, your grandpa began buying more and more land. But my sister still could not keep silent. She laughed at me because we had so many children.

What did she care? Did I ask for her help? No, I would never crawl to her. That is what she wanted to see. But I would rather suffer with your grandpa than crawl to her for help.

We had eleven children. Your mom was in the middle. What number? Oh, I do not remember now. There are so many. But I am not ashamed. Why should I be? There was another woman I knew in town who had sixteen children. She should be ashamed. But me? No, I have no reason to be embarrassed.

We worked hard and we owned our own rice mill. My life in the Philippines was good. I only came here because your mom needed me to help with your brother and you. I was not looking for a life in America. Why should I? My life is in the Philippines.

My mom, whom they named Ludivica, "Ludy" for short, was the seventh child of the eleven. Her siblings complained that she was the favorite after my grandfather named his rice mill after her, yet when it came time for my mom to go to college, my grandparents were adamant about not letting her go to Manila. Years earlier, my grandparents had sold plots of their land to put one of their older daughters through college in the city, only to find out later that she had eloped and had been pocketing all the money they were sending for her tuition. This ruined my mom's chances of ever going to college.

My mom begged and cried, promising that she would never do anything to betray them. "It's not fair!" she cried. "Why should I suffer for her mistake?"

"But it's like they had gambled and lost," my mom told me numerous times as I grew up. "They didn't want to gamble anymore."

Several months went by before my mom realized it was hopeless, and she prepared to live the rest of her life in Mindanao, helping her siblings and parents with the family business.

But then one day one of my mother's teachers, who was known as the town's fortune-teller, told my grandmother to let my mom go.

"If you let her, she will see America," she said.

A month later, through what was later regarded as divine intervention, my mom was off to National University in Manila, where she met my dad, Glorino.

Immediately after they graduated, my parents were married and prepared to leave for America. My mom was the first in the family to get a college degree, and the first to leave the Philippines. "I'll send for you," she told my weeping grandmother before she left.

Nine years later she did.

· · ·

When we got home from the airport, my mom showed my grandmother upstairs to her new room. We had just moved across town from our one-story house on Lexington Drive to a spacious four-bedroom house on Lomitas Drive to make room for Grandma Fausta. The former owners had painted each room a different pastel color. Grandma got the lime green room, next to my sky blue one.

I sat on her bed, watching her unpack. She brought out a picture and placed it on the dresser. "Who's that?" I asked.

"That's your cousin Riza," she said. "She was crowned the queen of Kiamba, the town where we're from."

I stared at that picture with envy for months. I examined the girl looking back at me with the powder white face atop a shiny brown neck. Bright pink eye shadow covered her lids, and her lips were smeared with the reddest lipstick I had ever seen. A white sash with the title "Miss Kiamba" was draped across her shimmering yellow dress. And right next to her was our grandfather with his arm around her.

"Grandma, is she his favorite?" I asked one day. I had expected her to respond the way typical grandmothers would—that they loved us all equally and that we were all special in our own way.

"Yes," she responded. "I think she is your grandpa's favorite. See how proud he looks?"

I hated my two-dimensional cousin after that. I hated her until years later when I met her in the Philippines and realized that she had grown up hating me for my life in America.

As for Grandma Fausta, she took to my brother instantly. He had the face of her sons and grandsons at home. She cradled him and sang him Filipino lullabies. When he got older, she spent hours in the kitchen preparing his favorite foods.

I had the face of my father. At eight years old, I was far less malleable than my infant brother. I was born in San Francisco and my latchkey American life was all I knew.

Her granddaughters my age in the Philippines had already been taught to cook and sew. I spent my summer climbing trees, playing with my dog, digging up worms, and skateboarding. Grandma Fausta had her concerns, but I quickly learned that communication was not one of her strengths; rather than talk to me, she used my one-year-old brother to convey her messages.

"Poor little Christopher," she said, as I stood right next to him. "Your sister doesn't act like a girl."

When I refused to eat her strange dishes, she picked up my brother and said, "I hope you don't eat like your sister when you grow up."

But I was a quick study, and I figured out how to play her game.

One day, as my grandmother was folding clothes, I stooped down next to my brother, who was playing by her side.

"Poor brother," I said. "Your grandmother is a mean old woman."

Before I could turn to look at her reaction, she slapped my arm and yelled, "You have no respect! You American! You're like sure!"

I didn't understand the last comment, but it was something she used repeatedly as I grew up. I knew it wasn't good.

My face burned with shame. But that was a turning point in our relationship. I learned that she wanted respect. She learned that it wouldn't be so easy.

• • •

Give me that mop! That will not get the floors clean. Come here and watch me.

You take a towel like this and put hot water and soap. Then you get on your hands and knees and wipe the floor like this. Do you think pushing that stick around will get out the dirt? That is for lazy people. We do not use those in the Philippines.

Now come here and wipe the floor the way I showed you. After you are done, I will show you how to wash the clothes by hand. Those machines will not take the dirt and sweat out. They will just dry the sweat and dirt deeper into the clothes.

Why do you look at me like that? You American. Children in the Philippines never look at their grandparents that way. You have no respect. God punishes children who look at their grandparents like that.

The next year was filled with little battles between my grandmother and me.

She saw every moment that I watched television, played outside, or stared out the window as signs of my idle nature. Her mission in America was to reprogram me.

Every day she insisted on showing me how to mop the floors, help her cook, clean the bathroom, sew, and do the laundry by hand. My hands became swollen and turned bright red, raw from the endless scrubbing. "Not clean enough!" she'd say. "You're being lazy."

I felt like I was in a boot camp, being taught the life of a generation and a culture so far removed from my own that I couldn't begin to understand it. I had stopped inviting my friends to the house for fear she would hand them a mop or toilet brush and put them to work.

The weekends were a blessing. My parents were home, and my grandmother wasn't nearly as demanding when they were around. She went about doing household chores, cooking, and playing with my brother.

I made the most of those days, trying to recapture the charmed life I'd led before she ever came into my world. The only benefit of her presence was that I could now leave the house—not that it was easy to escape her grueling chore schedule. I played outside and rode my bicycle until dusk, surrounding myself with the old imaginary friends I had plucked from television. I spent hours pretending I was part of an ultra-white suburban family. I played jacks on a square of extra linoleum my dad placed in the garage and sucked on popsicles, then watched television until it was time for bed. I lay on the family room floor eating peanut butter and jelly sandwiches with my feet up on the couch.

I often saw Grandma shooting an evil eye at me from the kitchen as she prepared vegetables, snapping green beans with a vengeance, expecting me to come and help. I stayed put, knowing she wouldn't say anything with my parents home.

But every Sunday she insisted that I attend Mass with her at St. James, the Catholic Church three blocks away from our house. I looked to my mom and dad for refuge. "She makes me do everything! She hates me!" I'd cry.

"Listen to your grandma," was all they would say.

I dragged out my morning routine, hoping she would grow frustrated and leave me behind. But she was there every time, waiting for me at the bottom of the stairs, her face a ghostly white from talcum powder and her lips stained with coral lipstick. She shook her head, watching me as I came downstairs.

"You take too long! You're making God wait!" she'd say, grabbing my wrist and pulling me along.

"But it's so boring in church!" I'd whine.

"Ay!" she'd reply in shock. "You have no shame! You American, you don't know anything about God. You're like sure!"

The hour of standing and sitting, kneeling and reciting

seemed like the cruelest, most unusual thing to do to a child. But it was during those Sunday Masses that I began to see another side of Grandma Fausta.

I looked over at her hands, small and weathered. The wrinkles stretched and intersected, like an intricate roadmap of her life. Her polished nails made for a strange dichotomy: soft, pearly pink tips, like oval shells atop the gravel and sandy terrain of her hands. Woven between her fingers were the dark ruby beads of her rosary.

After communion, she knelt and bowed her head. She closed her eyes so tight a crease formed in her forehead. It was always then that I saw her reach into her bag for the pale yellow handkerchief my cousin Riza had embroidered for her, using it to wipe the corners of her eyes. The choir was singing the communion song, number 215 in the blue book: "Here I am, Lord. Is it I, Lord? I have heard you calling in the night."

I couldn't imagine what she was asking from God—a better life, more patience, forgiveness for being cruel to me? Sometimes I thought she prayed I would be a better granddaughter.

When we got home, she went straight into her room and sang the loneliest tune I had ever heard. Her voice strained high and low, like an old violin struggling to find its melody. "What shall I do, what shall I do? My life is nothing without you." She sang that same line over and over.

I went into my room and put KC and the Sunshine Band on my old turntable, cranking up the volume until I could no longer hear the sadness from her room. Then I lay on my bed, staring at the wall where I had plastered posters of a young John Travolta, Donny and Marie Osmond, and Leif Garret, trying desperately to submerge myself in American pop culture.

"I think she misses the Philippines," I told my mom.

"Maybe we'll send for Grandpa, too," she said.

I believed that the power of God and religion were strong enough to draw out the shreds of kindness and sentimentality in Grandma Fausta. It was the Church's obligatory Sunday Mass that allowed me to witness that side of her, after all.

But one day, as I was walking past her bedroom, I caught a glimpse of her kneeling by her bed holding a familiar-looking book. I squinted to see the cover and noticed a symbol of the cross draped with lavender and yellow ribbons. Then it struck me—she had stolen the prayer book from church.

At the foot of her bed was her own personal stockpile of stolen prayer books. I wondered how she managed to dip her finger into the holy water every week without it sizzling on her flesh.

Chapter Two

Grandpa Paterno

God will always provide, so long as you are good. Of course, life has not always been easy, but I do not complain. You have to thank God and be grateful.

You are lucky, you know. Your mom and dad came to America for you so that you would never have to work in the rice fields or live a life in the provinces. Oh, how I love the Philippines, but that was the only life I knew. America, that is what you know and you have more opportunities here than any of your cousins in the Philippines. You are a lucky girl, do not forget that.

When your parents brought you to visit us in the Philippines, you were only four. Do you remember? You spoke Ilocano and wanted me to carry you all the time. "Lolo!" you'd cry. Do you remember? I always carried you, even if they told me you were already too big. I knew you would be leaving us soon.

Now you are growing so fast. Do not forget us, the old folks. We suffered for you. Your parents sacrificed for you. Remember that and live the life we all dreamed that you could have.

Grandpa Paterno was completely different from Grandma Fausta, and I was glad.

My mother had planned to send for her father first, to keep Grandma Fausta from being so lonely, but business at my Grandpa Sunday's rice mill was booming and it was too complicated for him to leave. "It's not time yet," he told my mom. So

Grandpa Paterno, my father's father, was the next to arrive.

My father couldn't send for relatives until he himself had become an American citizen, so it wasn't until after all the paperwork had cleared, in 1979—two years after Grandma Fausta had come to live with us—that Grandpa Paterno arrived. But it wasn't without complications.

Grandma was upstairs praying the rosary while the phone kept ringing. My mom and dad had left the house hours ago, saying they were going to pick up a surprise. "What is it?" I kept asking. "A really big surprise," my dad answered.

But it was dark outside now and they still had not returned.

"Hello?" I said as I picked up the phone, hoping it was my mom or dad.

"Hello? Hello?" said the man on the other line, sounding confused and tired. "This is Grandpa, Grandpa Paterno. I've been waiting at the airport for hours and nobody has come to get me."

I didn't know what to say. I didn't even know who he was.

"Who's that?" my dad asked, walking through the front door with a worried look on his face. My mom was behind him, frazzled and nervous.

"Some man who says he's Grandpa Paterno and that nobody came to get him," I answered.

"*Tatang! Adino ayan mo?* Dad, where are you?" my father asked after grabbing the phone from my hand. My mom was leaning forward, listening intently.

After he hung up, my dad told her they had marked down the wrong flight number and had to go back to the airport. By then it was 10:30 p.m. and the airport was nearly an hour away. "Just wait here," they told me.

"That was my first feeling when I came to America," Grandpa Paterno told me years later. "That nobody in America even cared to pick me up."

Early the next morning, the clanging of pots from the kitchen downstairs woke me. I stayed in bed for a while, knowing that

Grandma Fausta had chores waiting for me. But then the smell of garlic fried rice and *tapa*—fried strips of beef marinated in soy sauce, vinegar, and garlic—made its way up the stairs and into my room. My grumbling stomach fought with the rest of my lazy body and forced me to get up. I ran downstairs.

"Did you see your grandpa yet?" Grandma said.

"Where?" I answered.

"Upstairs, in the other room."

The "other room" was the sun gold room, next to Grandma's lime green one, across from the pink bathroom.

I went back upstairs, frightened of what was in store. I had just gotten used to Grandma Fausta, and I had fears that this grandparent was even worse.

I knocked softly on the door, hoping nobody would answer. "Come in," said the voice I had heard on the phone the night before.

I leaned forward, peeking through the small crack.

"*Neneng!*" my grandpa yelled, leaping from his bed. I didn't understand. ("It means my sweet young girl," he told me later.)

He hugged me tightly, then held me at arm's length, looking at my face and holding it with his two palms. His eyes began to well up with tears.

"You're so big now," he said. "When you came to the Philippines you were just a little baby."

Grandpa Paterno was a slender man who smelled of pomade and sandalwood soap. His thinning hair was combed neatly to the side. His smooth face was peppered with small black moles, and gray stubble shadowed his jawline. His brown eyes had specks of blue around their rims. I saw my dad in him, the same lips, the same eyes, the same kind and jovial manner.

I felt I had replaced my cousin Riza in that picture, and Grandpa Paterno had replaced Grandpa Domingo. Maybe it was because I had the face of his daughter and granddaughters back home. I didn't care why. At least with him I was the queen, the favorite.

• • •

Well, I am a quiet man. I don't talk much about myself, but I will tell you what you want to know.

I was born on May 25, 1919, in the very small Philippine town of Luna in the province of La Union. I was a soldier in World War II, fighting alongside American troops against the Japanese. You see here? This is a picture of me in my uniform. Handsome? You think so? Maybe, but I was just a young boy there. Of course I was frightened, but I had no choice. I left it in God's hands.

I was the second of nine children. I first saw your grandma with her friend sitting across from me in the town plaza. I thought she was quite beautiful. I was so shy, but I forced myself to go talk to her. I said, "Hi, I am Paterno." Then she stood up and walked away. I was so ashamed.

I asked her friend where she lived. Her house was so far away, but that night I walked on the dirt roads wearing my slippers and carrying my violin. I stood outside her house, serenading her until she appeared at her window.

"Go away!" she yelled. "You have no business here!"

I was so tired. My feet ached and my fingers were too tired to play. Silly? What is "silly"? I do not know that word. Do you mean foolish? No, I did not feel foolish. But I was in love. And they say that makes one a fool.

Your grandmother married me on May 4, 1944, and we moved to a very small home in the town of Bacnotan. Everyone called us "The Two Pats."

Your dad was born on February 5, 1945. Then there was Samuel, Delia, and Edgar.

From our home you could only see endless farmland. There was tobacco, coconuts, and many other vegetables. Only a small bit of land belonged to us, but that was enough. We grew rice on it.

We were very poor, but we always had enough. I did not have big dreams for myself, only to survive and provide for my family. Your dad was very bright. He was the one with dreams. He graduated valedictorian of his high school. He could have stayed with us in the province and worked on the land, but your grandma and I knew that was not the life he wanted. We asked all our relatives for help so that we could send him to college in Manila. Your grandma said he was our only hope for a better life. I did not need a better life, but I wanted it for him.

You see what happened? We sent him to National University in Manila and he graduated with a degree in industrial engineering. And now he is here in America. Without him, I would not have been able to come here. Now I can find a job and send for your grandma. Maybe we can even earn enough money to send some home to your cousins.

Grandpa Paterno's arrival was a blessing in many ways. His playful whistling had taken over my grandmother's sorrowful song, flooding our house with cheer.

He treated me with such care and adoration that Grandma Fausta felt compelled to play along. She began smiling and laughing more, carrying on as if she and I had spent the past two years having tea parties.

I wanted to tell my grandfather how mean she had been to me before he arrived. I wanted to tell my grandmother that I knew she was just pretending to like me so she wouldn't look so bad. But then our Sunday at church came along and I saw that she no longer cried as she knelt and prayed. Maybe, I thought, she had been asking God for someone to talk to.

"Abalayan" they called each other. It was a term of endearment for in-laws, for which there is no translation in English.

In the morning they sat at the breakfast table after my parents left for work. Grandpa Paterno drank coffee while Grandma Fausta made her tea. She took out fresh *pan de sal* (Filipino rolls) from the oven and placed them on the table.

They spent a good hour talking—about the Philippines, about America, about how everything was so different here. She tried to prepare him for the culture shock, something no one had done for her. In America, she explained, everyone works. When you're old, nobody pays attention.

In the Philippines, there was always something to do and somewhere to go. There were *trikes* (rickshaws), *jeepneys* (converted jeeps used as taxis), and various other modes of cheap transportation to take you to public markets and shopping malls. Relatives were always coming in and out of the house, checking on each other and just keeping each other company.

"Not here, Abalayan," she said. "Here, you are alone."

Her warning didn't seem to affect Grandpa Paterno. He began helping her around the house, allowing me to be a kid again. I was grateful for the new sounds—their conversations, his tunes, Grandma Fausta's laughter.

I spent endless hours with my grandpa, picking tomatoes in the vegetable garden or taking walks. He wasn't a talkative man, but he had an easy way about him that allowed me to say whatever I wanted. He listened and smiled, offering advice when I asked, or words of encouragement when he thought I needed it.

"Be good in school, Neneng," he'd say. "Make us all proud."

One morning as I got up for school, I saw Grandpa Paterno in his room dressed to go out. He was sitting on his bed, bent down tying his shoelaces.

"Are you walking me to school today?" I asked.

"No, Neneng. I'm going to work. I got a job!"

He was filled with excitement, but I was completely devastated.

I remembered Grandma Fausta's words: *Here in America, everyone works.*

I had come to think that Grandma was here for my brother, and Grandpa was here for me. Now that he would be going to work like my parents, who would be my designated grandparent? I began to panic, wondering if Grandma Fausta would go back to her former self.

I ran into my room and slammed the door, throwing myself dramatically on the bed and crying into my pillow.

"Why are you crying?" my grandpa asked, walking into the room. "What is bothering you?"

Grandma Fausta came out of her room and stood in my doorway.

"I don't want you to go! I don't want you to work!" I screamed.

He let out a little chuckle and stroked my hair.

"You know, Neneng, I came here to earn money. Your cousins in the Philippines don't have the life you have here. Don't you want me to help them? And your Grandma Patricia is waiting for me to send for her. If I work hard, soon she will be here too."

After Grandpa Paterno started working, Grandma Fausta took pity on me. It was then that she and I began having our own small conversations—not about housework but about her life, and what she had hoped for mine.

I didn't know if it was because of Grandpa Paterno or because she had simply become accustomed to her new life, but something had changed. She still wasn't Mary, Betty, or Alice, but she had found a way to become my grandmother.

Grandpa Paterno promised he would be home every day before dinner. He had taken a job as a busboy at a local diner. He always came home with a treat wrapped in paper towel for me: fried chicken, biscuits, cookies. My favorites were the small packs of honey, which I'd slit open and savor while Grandpa Paterno told me about his day or memories from the Philippines.

He often told me the story of my father's fight with a water buffalo.

The large animals were abundant in their province and were sometimes used for plowing. Once, Grandpa Paterno said, my dad grew infuriated when one of the buffalos refused to move. My dad threw his hat off and kicked the animal in its rear. He ranted and raved for a good while before my grandpa finally stopped laughing and went over to calm him down.

I was reminded of this story years later when it was Grandpa Paterno who stepped in and calmed everyone down during a family crisis. It was he who kept our family from falling completely apart.

• • •

Summer had arrived and our backyard was ripe for the picking. On the left side of the house I plucked blackberries bursting with sweet nectar from their thorny vines. Grandma Fausta shook the branches of our almond tree and watched the nuts drop into the straw basket she was carrying. Figs and pears had to be gathered from the ground since our trees had yielded so much fruit that year.

I filled bowls with cherry tomatoes from the garden and sat under the sun dipping the small fruits into a little heap of salt and savoring the mix of flavors. Grandma Fausta hung clothes from a line of rope she had strung from the house to the fence, once again ignoring the washer and dryer in the laundry room. I sat under the freshly washed clothes, looking up at the white sheets flapping in the warm breeze and taking in the scent of the season. I loved summer vacation.

During one of these lazy afternoons, my mom came home early from work. I heard the sliding door open and saw her turning her head from side to side. I was hidden between the apple tree and the fence that separated our backyard from the sidewalk and a main road. Sometimes I peeked through a small hole and spied on white people walking by, imagining what their lives were like and how wonderfully normal they were compared to mine.

"Pati!" Mom yelled. I ran toward the house to greet her. "I have a surprise," she said. "We're going to Disneyland!"

I let out a screech and jumped up and down. I had never been to the magical place that I had seen on television. It all seemed so American. I imagined Grandpa Paterno carrying me on his shoulders as we went from one attraction to the next. I pictured us spinning in teacups and holding hands with Mickey Mouse.

"Grandma Fausta will come with us so she can help with you and your brother. Grandpa Paterno can't come because he has to work," she said.

My heart sank. Grandma Fausta wasn't as bad as she was before Grandpa Paterno had arrived, but she wasn't exactly my first choice for an amusement park companion either. This was supposed to be my summer vacation trip. I didn't need her bringing me down with stories about how my poor cousins in the Philippines didn't have a Disneyland where they lived.

I let out a moan. "Does she *have* to come?" I asked, rolling my eyes and hunching my back.

"You act like that and no one will go at all," my mom answered.

The next morning, we packed our van with blankets, an ice chest full of snacks and drinks, and bags of clothes. It was going to be a road trip. A full day of listening to Grandma Fausta complain about her dizziness and arthritis. A full day of feeling her shrewd eyes watching every move I made. A full day of pure hell just to get to the "Happiest Place on Earth." I couldn't wait until school started.

After we checked into our hotel, I begged to go to Disneyland right away. We only had one day to spend there since my mom and dad planned to visit their friends who lived nearby, so I wanted to make the most of our time. Grandma Fausta glared at me. She wanted to lie down and rest, but I couldn't care less. "Please!" I cried until my dad finally gave in.

When we got to the front gate, I stared at all the beautiful flowers and the fairy-tale buildings that lined the pathways. I thought I was in heaven. I wanted to go on every ride and see every attraction. The lines were all long and the park was packed, but it didn't bother me. I was in Disneyland, a place that had no trace of the Philippines. I stared in awe at all the mechanical dolls singing "It's a Small World" in different languages, praying that I wouldn't hear the language of my grandparents coming from their mouths.

We were just about to go to the Haunted Mansion when Grandma Fausta began to limp.

"Apay?" my mom asked. "What's wrong?"

Grandma said her hip was hurting because she wasn't used to standing in long lines and walking so much.

"We have to go back to the room now," my dad said. "Your

grandma has to rest."

I burst into tears, wondering why she'd even had to come at all. "But I want to see the haunted house!" I screamed.

Suddenly, I felt a sharp, painful pinch on my arm. I looked over and saw my mom, whose eyes had narrowed and were staring at me with the same terrifying look that Grandma Fausta had perfected.

"Don't you care that your grandma doesn't feel good?" she asked. I stopped crying, feeling more defeated than angry.

I would have preferred to stay home eating cherry tomatoes in the backyard than have Grandma Fausta ruin my first trip to Disneyland. But I had no choice. It was time to go home.

Chapter Three

The Move

Shortly after the New Year marking the beginning of the 1980s, my parents decided it was time to buy a new house.

They had heard about a suburb an hour away where many Filipino families were buying homes. While Grandma Fausta and Grandpa Paterno had kept each other company, our family was very much an island in our Livermore community. At the time, I was the only minority at my elementary school and I was constantly teased and taunted.

During a field trip to the Oakland Museum, a boy on the school bus stood up and said, "Look, those are your people!" pointing to a black family outside. Everyone turned and laughed at me.

"I'm not black!" I yelled.

"Yes you are, and your lips are this big!" he screamed, opening his mouth as wide as he could. Everyone on the bus burst into laughter as my face burned with humiliation and self-hatred.

"Thank God they don't know Grandma Fausta," I thought.

The next day, in an effort to teach the class a valuable lesson in cultural sensitivity, my teacher surprised me by calling me to the front of the room.

"Pati is what you call a fil-ip-PEE-no, class. Can you say that?"

I felt myself physically shrinking.

"Maybe you can bring the class some fil-ip-PEE-no food later this week so they know what kinds of things *your* family eats," she said, smiling, completely ignorant of the fact that she had only made me more of a freak.

When I got home, I rummaged through the kitchen, not exactly knowing what was fil-ip-PEE-no food and what was "normal." I didn't want to bring any of the weird, smelly stuff that Grandma Fausta made every night, so I grabbed a bag of pork rinds that my mom had bought from the supermarket.

"This is what *my* people eat," I said the next day, holding up the bag of Granny Goose pork rinds.

"Hey! My dad eats Filipino food every day!" one of the boys yelled out.

"That's it," my mom said after the teacher called to tell her what happened. "We're moving." Nobody was happier than Grandma Fausta. For months she had complained that she couldn't find any ingredients for her Filipino dishes since there were no Asian markets.

One afternoon as we were all packing, Grandma Fausta asked my parents if our dog, Yober, would be coming with us. She told them she couldn't hang her laundry outside because he constantly grabbed the sheets with his teeth and pulled them off. "He's so big and his fur is everywhere," she complained.

I wasn't paying too much attention because I knew my parents would naturally bring Yober along. He was my babysitter before the Oracles arrived, after all. He was family.

But that night when my dad came to say goodnight, he sat on my bed and told me Yober would not be coming. He was too big, he said, and Grandma Fausta was afraid of him.

"But he's not mean to anyone!" I yelled. "She's the mean one. She should be the one not moving with us!"

I pounded on my mattress with my fist, overwhelmed by anger and panic. Yober cared for me and looked out for me every day when I was alone. We'd shared countless afternoons playing on our backyard lawn with a tennis ball. I soaked my pillow with tears that night and went to school the next day with my eyes practically swollen shut. When I got home, Yober was already gone.

We moved into a smaller home with a master bedroom and two bedrooms upstairs, and another downstairs. Grandma Fausta took the larger room next to mine, and Grandpa Paterno settled in downstairs.

The rooms seemed strange with the bare white walls. No colors, no identity, no history. "It's plain!" I whined as I walked around the new house. "It's a new beginning," Grandpa Paterno answered.

A few months after we moved into the home in Vallejo, Grandma Fausta prepared for a two-week vacation to the Philippines. She hadn't seen her husband or her other children and grandchildren in over three years. Grandpa Paterno had not yet found a job in the area, so he was able to stay home with my brother and me.

I saw these two weeks as a vacation as well. Grandma Fausta had eased her expectations of me after Grandpa Paterno arrived, but her presence always carried the weight of Catholic guilt. I felt it was my solemn duty to help carry out her daily chores, lest I be sentenced to eternal suffering.

During her absence, Grandpa Paterno taught me how to ride the new bike I got for Christmas. He also made traditional dishes like *adobo,* a pork and chicken stew, and a provincial dish called *dinengdeng,* fried fish placed on top of an array of vegetables—eggplant, Chinese bitter melon, okra, green beans, bamboo shoots—all boiled in an anchovy broth. In return, I showed him the joy of waffles for breakfast and peanut butter and jelly sandwiches for lunch. Two weeks seemed like two days. Before I knew it, Grandma Fausta was on her way back, and she wasn't alone.

Chapter Four

Grandpa Sunday

My English no good. You ask me questions English, I answer you Ilocano. You understand Ilocano, but you not speak it good, right? You and me, we talk this way, okay? We start now.

I followed Grandpa Sunday closely as he spoke in Ilocano, asking him to slow down and repeat things here and there as my mind raced to translate his words.

Where is Payless? Someone come home to Philippines and show me picture in front of Payless. I want job there. I like go working.

I am farmer. I have many land in Philippines. I am carpenter. I make furniture, you give me wood and sharp knife. I am fisherman. I love music. Your Grandma say I buy too many things. That is why I work, for money, to buy things.

No favorite kids. I love them all the same. When I die, I will leave them all equal share of my land. That is fair. I work hard all my life. Now I want to enjoy before I die. Your grandma, she is serious. I play jokes and she gets mad, but I make her laugh.

Do not mind her so much when she yells at you. That is her way. That is how she was taught to live. She wants you to learn and work hard like she did. She no like lazy. She raise eleven kids, she does not know how to relax. How do I know how to relax? I was on land farming while she inside yelling at kids.

· · ·

The whole family packed into the van—Mom, Dad, my brother, Grandpa Paterno, and me. Grandma Fausta's flight was arriving at San Francisco Airport at 6:30 p.m. through PAL, Philippine Airlines. My dad always said PAL stood for "Plane Always Late."

My brother had grown very attached to Grandma Fausta, calling out for her and crying often while she was away. By now he was four years old and quite capable of throwing a tantrum. "Mama!" he'd scream. "Where's Mama?" He'd stare out the window looking out into the street, waiting for her to come home.

We sat on the black chairs outside her terminal. I was reminded of when she first came to America and how different she had been from what I'd expected. I looked for that same face among the people appearing from the 747.

"There's Mama!" my brother screamed. I looked up to find her but was surprised yet again at what I saw. She had gotten a haircut and done away with her tightly wound bun. I had expected her to be miserable coming back to America, but she looked years younger and was glowing. She made her way through the crowd, waving to us the whole time.

"Your grandpa is here now!" she said, practically singing. "Your Grandpa Domingo is here!"

There behind her was a tall, handsome man with a red ball cap. His large ears poked out beneath the sides of his hat. He had a playful grin like a little boy who just gotten a new toy. Beneath his dark-rimmed glasses I could see my mother's eyes.

He and my mom embraced. *"Papang,"* she said softly as she buried her face in his chest and began to cry.

Years later, my brother asked what "Domingo" meant. "Sunday," Grandma Fausta replied. And from then on, he was always known as Grandpa Sunday.

Though he settled into our house and got along well with the other Oracles, I never formed a close bond with Grandpa Sunday. He easily grew frustrated when he couldn't find the right English words to form a sentence, and I was just as impatient when I struggled to find the right Ilocano words. So we politely avoided being alone together, using Grandma Fausta as a translator whenever we felt the need to communicate.

Unlike my other grandparents, he never told me stories of his past, the language barrier between us preventing him from doing so. To me, he was my grandmother's husband and my mother's father. I never felt like he was my grandfather, nor I his granddaughter.

• • •

Each of them had added something different to my life—Grandma Fausta, discipline; Grandpa Paterno, love; Grandpa Sunday, laughter. I didn't feel like anything was missing. But Grandpa Paterno did.

"How I wish your other grandma was here already," he often said. A few months later, his wish came true.

"Oh no," my mom whispered when we got the news that my Grandma Patricia would be arriving.

"What's wrong?" I asked.

She shook her head and waved her hand, which meant it was none of my concern. I would soon find out that it was not only my concern, but that of our whole family.

Chapter Five

Grandma Patricia

*Do you see the hairs on my arm standing? Oh, I am so cold. That
means there is a ghost nearby. I will get my rosary and pray to my
Santo Niño to protect me before I sleep. Barree, barree, barree. That is
what I say to keep the evil spirits away. Are you not afraid? There are
spirits all around you. That is why I always keep my statues of the
Santo Niño and the Virgin Mary close to my bed as I sleep. Without
them, I dream that so many evil spirits are circling around me. Do not
laugh. You must learn to believe.*

By now I was a pro. When my parents said we were going to the
airport, I knew exactly what that meant—another grandparent
was coming.

I had practically memorized the route from the parking
garage to the Philippine Airlines terminal. We'd take the eleva-
tor to the second floor, follow the signs, ride an escalator, go
straight, then turn left.

This time it was only my parents, Grandpa Paterno, and me
who waited at the airport. My brother and Grandpa Sunday
stayed home with Grandma Fausta so she could cook a meal
for Grandma Patricia's arrival. Before we left the house, she had
already brought out a big bag of green beans, preparing them
for the pot of *dinengdeng* and *kare-kare*, an oxtail stew in rich
peanut broth with eggplant, bok choy, and green beans.

I didn't give much thought to this grandmother's arrival.
Unlike with the others, I wasn't caught by surprise. Grandpa
Paterno had tried to prepare me during the drive to the airport.

"She's short and thin," he said. "She carried you a lot when you were little and your mom and dad took you to the Philippines for vacation. Don't you remember?"

He searched my face, hoping that somehow he had successfully jogged my memory. But I was only four years old when my parents took me back to the Philippines.

Sometimes there would be scenes in my head that I could never quite place. I was walking down a narrow stairway with change in my hand. Someone told me to catch up with a street peddler to buy *santol*, a large, round, sour fruit that was pickled and salted. But the peddler had already turned the corner with his cart and I couldn't catch up. I remembered feeling sad and crying because I had been craving the tartness of the fruit.

In another scene, I was standing outside of an old house made of cement. I was too short to look into a window, so I climbed on some cinderblocks. I saw an old piece of soap on the sill and tried to reach out to touch it right before I lost my balance and fell. A woman picked me up and took me in the house. My knee was bleeding and she rubbed some leaves on it. I remembered that it had stung and that I screamed.

"Yes! That was your Grandma Patricia!" Grandpa said, after I retold the story. "That was your auntie's house and she was rubbing bitter melon leaves on your cut so it would stop bleeding."

Up until then, those scenes were like dreams—ageless, meaningless, and haunting.

I thought I had seen it all, but I wasn't prepared for Grandma Patricia's arrival. When my dad spotted her in the terminal, he let out a yell and she immediately burst into tears. It was different from when my mom cried at the sight of Grandpa Sunday.

Grandma Patricia was sobbing. I didn't know if she was happy or if someone had forced her to get on the plane. "What's wrong with her?" I whispered to my mom. "Shh!" she replied, pinching my arm.

After crying inconsolably on my grandpa's shoulder, she moved on to my dad, crying even more. I began to shrink as people at the airport turned to stare at us. I wanted to stand somewhere else and pretend I was with another family, one whose grandmother wasn't causing such a scene.

Finally she turned to my mom, hugging her and saying words I couldn't understand under all the sniffling. *"Daytoy ni Pati,"* my mom said, putting her arm around me. "Here is Pati."

And then she began to wail, a deep, sorrowful, soulful sound that gave me the chills and made the hairs on my arms stand. It was a sound brought over from another place and time, where people longed and suffered and worshipped and rejoiced. It was all of those things in one powerful expression.

She grabbed me tightly with both arms and released all of her emotions. I felt her tears falling on my neck and her warm breath as she spoke. I didn't know what she was saying, or if she was even talking to me. It was as if she was chanting or praying.

If I had the power, I would have turned and run away, but I was frozen. I didn't know what to say or do. So we stood there, together—a Filipino grandmother and her American name-sake—for what seemed like an eternity.

. . .

There's a saying among some Filipinos that we are all like crabs in a barrel—grabbing onto each other to get to the top, then letting go of those behind us and pushing them back before we crawl out. When Grandma Fausta came to America, Grandma Patricia had viewed her as the crab that made it out. She harbored her resentment and jealousy until it was her turn to crawl out of the barrel.

The analogy was always an interesting one to me. If a crab was forced to stay in the barrel too long, I wondered, would it eventually go bad?

Patricia Membrere was born on March 17, 1925, in Bacnotan, La Union. She was younger than her four siblings: Paulina,

Lorenzo, Hermegilda, and Filomena. Of the five, she was the only one who graduated from high school and she was preparing to go to college until she met Grandpa and got married. She spent all of her married life as a housewife, helping Grandpa around the small farm, but mostly raising their four children.

Grandma Patricia had a beautiful singing voice. She and Grandpa Paterno would often spend the warm, humid nights on their porch singing together while Grandpa played the guitar. Their voices filled the air and met in the treetops, harmonizing and calling out to the neighbors.

She relied heavily on Grandpa, and he was always there to take care of her and comfort her when she needed it. "Where will you ever find another man like your grandpa?" she would say to me.

Bacnotan was one of the more primitive towns in the Philippines and Grandma was brought up on old wives' tales, superstition and, at times, black magic.

In her household, certain herbs, soups, and dishes could be used for various things—to welcome or ward off spirits, prolong life, or help fertility. Photographs, articles of clothing, and other personal objects were used to bring good luck or misfortune to someone. Nobody believed she practiced the black magic herself, but she knew how it was done, and who to go to if she ever required such services.

Her life seemed to be a contradiction in many ways. While she believed in black magic, she was also deeply religious, attending Catholic Mass several times a week and praying to the Santo Niño, the Baby Jesus. And though she was religious, she was also very liberal in areas the Church often was not.

At a time when sex was not openly spoken about, let alone contraception, Grandma Patricia would hand out condoms in the village in an effort to teach young people about birth control. She had begun volunteering at a small clinic, where condoms were available. Nobody would take them, too ashamed and shocked at the very thought.

Perhaps her biggest contradiction was her relationship with my mother. My dad had written to her from college that he had a new girlfriend from Kiamba named Ludy Baigan and that he would be bringing her home to meet the family. The day before they arrived, Grandma was introduced to some people at a gathering who said they were from the same town, and when my grandmother asked them if they had heard of the Baigan family, they were overjoyed. They told Grandma that the Baigans were one of the most respected families in Kiamba, and that their business had also made them one of the richest.

When my dad arrived with my mom, Grandma was waiting on the porch to greet them. She jumped to her feet when she saw their car drive down the muddy pathway. My mom stepped out in her small heels and my grandma rushed to wipe the mud from them. She served her sweetened tea and rice cakes with coconut wrapped in banana leaves.

My mom thought she had made a great impression. She didn't know that Grandma had long placed her dreams of a better life on my father's shoulders. The college education she was supposed to have was now his. The success he would achieve would become hers.

When my parents decided to get married right after they graduated, my grandmother was heartsick. "Don't get angry if Glorino sends us money. We will be expecting it from him," she told my mom before they left for America.

My mom knew Grandma held her responsible for taking her son away. When I was born, she named me after her, hoping that would soften her mother-in-law's feelings toward her. And now that she would be coming to America more than a decade later maybe they could start over, my mom thought.

Grandma Patricia was the last crab to crawl out of the barrel. She had been left too long, and I wondered later if she had already gone bad.

• • •

Though Grandma Patricia was the youngest of the four, she was the oldest soul. She had created a makeshift altar in her room with a statue of the Santo Niño, a crucifix, a picture of the Virgin Mary, and an array of rosaries. Every day she would place fresh fruit or flowers at the feet of Baby Jesus.

"They will chase the evil away," she would say. I couldn't imagine what evil spirits lurked in the confines of our subdivision. I found Grandma Patricia strange and fascinating.

By then I was eleven years old, just starting the sixth grade, my last year before middle school. I was nearing the age when I was too cool for my parents, let alone four grandparents all under the same roof. But Grandma Patricia's eccentricities were enough to keep me a kid just a little bit longer.

For every ailment, Grandma had a homespun cure. Once, when I woke up with an eye infection, she was convinced she knew the cause and that the only way to get rid of it was to drop human urine into my eye.

"No!" I screamed as she insisted I pee in a cup and rub the liquid in my eye. "You're crazy! I won't do it!" I yelled, convinced that she belonged in a supervised facility.

"You do not believe, but I know!" she fought back. She insisted that the swelling would go down, but I ran upstairs and locked myself in the bathroom. With all the talk about urine, I really had to go. I rushed to the toilet and released all the pressure.

"Ahh, good. I hear you are urinating. You listened to me. Good girl," said Grandma Patricia with her head pressed up against the other side of the door.

"Go away!" I screamed. "I won't leave this bathroom until you leave me alone! You're crazy!"

Another time, when a rash had spread all over my body after I ate one of her dishes, she covered me with strange oils and powder and began chanting *barree, barree, barree...* rolling her Rs. I lay there, tarred and feathered, wondering if she had gone completely mad.

When Grandma Patricia was with the other Oracles, she

laughed and smiled, telling stories and hugging Grandma
Fausta. But in her room, she was always very serious. She
looked me in the eye and said that I should never forget where I
came from. That even though I was born in America, my blood
and soul were born of the mountains, the fields, the muddy
rice paddies of the Philippines. "You are not as different as you
think," she said. She was right.

Grandma Patricia had a gift for writing. She composed the
most beautiful letters, filled with style and sentiment. Sometimes her eyes grew weak and she asked me to make sure her
writing was legible. Her penmanship was artful and her English
was textbook.

"God has brought me here to be with your *Manang* Pati," she
wrote to one of my cousins in the Philippines. "Manang" was
a term of respect for older sister or older female cousin. "With
God's grace, your Grandpa and I can earn money and help
everyone at home. Be studious, and be kind."

I was moved by these words, and though Grandma Patricia
was the most unusual and complex of the four, I felt that I had
found my kindred spirit.

Chapter Six

The Honeymoon

With Grandma Patricia in place, the Oracles were complete. For the next couple of months, they all enjoyed a honeymoon period, where every day was like a party. They gathered in the kitchen, cooking and eating, then congregated in the patio under the flickering shade of trees. I couldn't wait to get home from school to take refuge in all the festivity and communion.

Grandma Patricia sang and danced for everyone. Other times Grandpa Sunday brought down his shiny new silver boombox and played the latest cassette tapes he had bought, mostly country music. On the weekends, when everyone was home, I practiced my piano lessons, playing my favorite song, "The Last Waltz," from the red lesson book. It was a simple piece, but every time I played it Grandma Patricia and Grandpa Paterno used our tiled foyer as their ballroom and danced.

My parents seemed happy as well. Every day when they came home from work a banquet of hot, traditional dishes was waiting at the table. The rice cooker was placed in the middle, steam swirling from the fresh batch. We ate dinner at the same time, all eight of us, grabbing stools and lawn chairs so that we could all be seated at the table together.

The Oracles ate with their hands; *kamet* they would call it. I felt like I was eating with cave people. I stole glances at them, careful not to let them see me.

They used the four fingers of their right hands to scoop up

the rice and vegetables, then used their thumbs to push the food forward and into their mouths. I suppose it was a necessity before utensils and chopsticks were invented, but I couldn't understand the need to carry on this tradition.

Still, I always placed a spoon and fork next to their plates. And for years they went back in the drawer, unused.

There was always fish at the table—*bangus*, or "milkfish," mackerel, catfish, flounder, or tilapia. After dinner, they snapped the individual fish bones from the naked spine and use them for toothpicks. The first time I saw them do this I couldn't believe it. It was a scene straight out of *The Flintstones*.

"We have toothpicks here," I said, bringing out the box.

"Wasting trees," Grandpa Paterno replied. They broke into laughter.

Dinner was never quite the same.

· · ·

No honeymoon would be complete without a trip. One weekend, my dad suggested we all get into the van and drive to Reno, Nevada. None of my grandparents had ever been in a casino before, and downtown Reno was filled with them.

Reno was a two-and-half-hour drive from our home—the first road trip for our new extended family. There were frequent stops, as one would imagine with four seniors packed into a van. Unfortunately, my grandparents had not learned how to synchronize their bathroom schedules, so we stopped at every rest area, and many gas stations in between.

My dad looked at my grandparents in the rearview mirror, telling them how slot machines worked.

"If you see three of the same thing on the line, then you hit the jackpot," he said. "If you're lucky, you can turn one quarter into thousands of dollars."

My grandparents listened in awe. Their eyes widened with my dad's last statement.

"Could you imagine," Grandma Patricia said, "how many Philippine pesos those thousands of dollars would be?"

"I buy car!" Grandpa Sunday jumped in.

"Ay! Car! You can't even get a license!" yelled Grandma Fausta.

Everyone burst into laughter, but I felt sorry for him. I knew what it felt like to be at the receiving end of her criticisms. I looked at him, sticking out my lower lip in a sign of support.

Spotting my encouragement, he said: "I buy American car. Bring to Kiamba. Only one with American car."

"You're like sure," Grandma said, to which everyone laughed, including Grandpa Sunday.

My grandparents stared out the window as the van climbed its way up the winding two-way road through the mountains. My grandparents had also never seen snow, and the mountains and trees there were covered with it. "You see," Grandma Patricia said, turning to me. "The hairs on my arm are standing because it is so beautiful."

I looked out the window at a view I had seen several times before. But the snow looked different to me now—fresh, white, crisp, and sparkling.

"Can we stop?" I asked my dad. I wanted to get out and play in it. My mom told my dad to pull over. We were at a high elevation and the view was breathtaking.

My brother and I jumped out before the van had even stopped. He began making snowballs.

"Be careful!" screamed Grandma Fausta. "Does it hurt?"

At first they were all afraid to touch the snow. They simply stared at it in amazement, poking at it then moving away.

"It's just ice," I said to them. "See?" I formed a snowball and threw it at Grandpa Sunday. He was my safest target since he was the most playful and least frightened. The other three screamed, as if I had just dropped a valuable vase.

In a sense, I suppose it *was* valuable. In the Philippines, ice was a commodity, and in the provinces where my grandparents came from, it was even harder and more expensive to come by.

None of them had owned freezers to make and store it, so they bought it at local stores or ice houses.

Grandpa Sunday stuck his arms elbow-deep into a pile of snow, determined to get me back. He chased me around, ready to hurl his ammunition. All the while I could hear my grandmothers yelling in the background: "You're going to fall!" "Ay!" "You will break your neck!"

Grandpa Sunday, breaking a sweat, threw the snowball at my back, watching it explode like a powdered-sugar firework. He bent down, placing his hands on his knees to catch his breath.

"You see! Now you are too tired! You will get sick!" yelled Grandma Fausta.

Grandpa Sunday lifted his head and looked at me with a big grin. "Your grandma. Too serious."

After all of our stops, we arrived in Reno more than three hours later. By then the sun had begun to set and the lights of the casinos shone like a beacon before us. I could hear my grandparents gasp as our van made it over the final hill, the road giving way to the brilliant structures on the horizon.

We drove under the city's trademark sign—an arch stretching from one side of the street to the other with the words "Reno, The Biggest Little City in the World" in flashing lights. They each craned their necks and tilted their heads as we passed underneath it. I could see the reflection of the lights on the lenses of their eyeglasses.

I was more interested in watching their reaction than being in Reno. The best things the city had to offer for me were its buffets and arcades, although I also profited from my parents' winnings. Whenever either of them won, I would get a handful of shiny silver dollars, which I'd store away in an old sock in my drawer.

"Maybe I can win, Neneng," Grandpa Paterno said to me. Up until then, he had not said much—of the four, he was content to stay quietly in the background—but he had the same stars in his eyes. Just like the rest of them, the list of possibilities was running through his mind: What if I hit the jackpot? What if I go home with thousands of dollars? What if I can finally send money to those in the Philippines?

The sounds of ringing, shuffling, and spinning surrounded us as we entered the casino. The air was thick with cigarette smoke and cheap alcohol. My grandmothers held on to one another, walking slowly as if they were crossing a busy street. The grandfathers looked from one end of the room to the other at the sea of slots, roulette wheels, and green-felt card tables.

Grandpa Sunday, always intrigued by machinery, was ready to drop his coins, but the other three looked crestfallen, like their fantasy of the American Dream had just been spoiled. What they saw was greed, waste, sin, and desperation.

My grandmothers said they would stay in the hotel room with my brother and me, refusing to become gambling heathens like the rest. But my parents convinced them that the trip would be a waste if they didn't pull the lever of at least one slot machine.

My mom handed each grandparent one hundred dollars to play with, except for Grandma Patricia, to whom she gave one hundred and fifty. I looked at the others, who didn't seem to care or notice, and then at Grandma Patricia, who gave a little smile and tucked the cash into her coat pocket.

After we settled into our room, Dad took my brother and me to the arcade while my mom served as a gambling mentor to the Oracles. We agreed to meet at the buffet for dinner after two hours. Before we separated, each of my grandparents touched my brother's hand, as if his youthful innocence would bring them luck. As they walked away, I heard a faint sound from Grandma Fausta's side pocket, and I knew it was from the beads of her rosary. I didn't know if she'd brought God into the casino to help her win or to save her from the heresy of it all. She held on tightly to Grandma Patricia's arm.

By the end of the night, my grandmothers had each played and lost fifty cents and decided that was enough for them. When I saw them walking toward the restaurant two hours later, they were still clinging to each other—crabs in a barrel.

Mom stood with her arms folded, surveying the main floor for the two grandpas. She had left them sitting side by side at the quarter slot machines, each with a bucket of coins on his lap. I went over to my grandmothers, who had found a spot on a wooden bench and were speaking in hushed tones.

I knew enough Ilocano to understand that they hated Reno and they wanted to go home. Grandma Fausta felt sick from inhaling all the smoke, and Grandma Patricia felt she was surrounded by evil. I grew irritated listening to them take turns complaining.

"There!" my mom yelled, pointing in front of her. I looked up to see Grandpa Sunday running toward us with two large plastic cups filled with coins. "I win!" he yelled. "I win!" Grandpa Paterno was behind him, carrying two other cups that held the surplus of Grandpa Sunday's winnings. Grandma Fausta and Grandma Patricia quickly freed themselves from each other, jumped up, and ran toward him. "I win!" Grandpa Sunday kept yelling.

Retelling the story, he had already lost fifty dollars and was about to stop when he dropped two quarters into a slot machine on the way to the restaurant. "Three seven! Three seven!" he said, demonstrating the spin and jackpot on an invisible slot machine in front of him.

"Abalayan, *balato,*" Grandma Patricia said. Mom explained that some Filipinos believe that when you win you must give something back so the good fortune will continue. Grandma Patricia was reminding Grandpa that it was time to give back.

When Grandpa Sunday returned from cashing in his coins, he handed each of us twenty dollars and volunteered to pay for dinner. He smiled all night, and of the four, he was the only one who ever gambled again.

"I like Reno," he repeated on the way home. "I go back again."

Chapter Seven

In the Middle

After the honeymoon, the Oracles established daily routines around the house.

Grandma Fausta continued to cook most of the meals and took care of my brother. Grandma Patricia was in charge of cleaning and doing the laundry. Grandpa Sunday tended to the yardwork and used his lifelong farming skills on his own modest vegetable garden. Grandpa Paterno was everyone's assistant, helping with everything—cooking, cleaning, childcare, and gardening.

Where would I ever find a man like Grandpa Paterno, I wondered.

At thirteen, when I started middle school, things for me became far more complicated. I had been looking forward to starting middle school all summer. I'd heard about how everybody dressed and spoke and wore their hair. At the time, "knickers," also known as "pedal pushers," and Mary Jane shoes were in. Boys were wearing baggy pants with pleats all along the waist and black leather jackets that formed a V in the back. And everyone, no matter girl or boy, had a Members Only jacket and a pair of Dickies and Ben Davis pants.

It was 1981, and MTV had become my window to pop culture. Everything was loud—music, hair, makeup, personalities. I was emerging as a teenager at a time when music videos and VJs were revolutionizing the way people looked, acted, and dressed. I couldn't wait to make my debut.

When I got my upcoming class schedule in the mail, I ripped the envelope open and jumped on my bed, shouting and laughing. I couldn't wait to get a locker, to have five different classes with five different teachers and sets of classmates.

My grandmothers yelled for me to stop, saying that I wasn't acting like a young lady. But I couldn't contain my excitement. Like the fresh white walls of our new home, this school was a blank canvas, ripe with promise.

But when the day came, after I finished taking a shower I saw laid out on my bed a red and white T-shirt from the Philippines with a picture of a little girl's face staring back at me. Grandma Patricia had brought it for me as a gift when she came to America, and I had thought it made a cute pajama top. On the girl's head was a pink hat with bright red yarn braided and sewn onto it to look like hair.

Grandma had placed the matching skirt below it—large red and pink horizontal ruffles and the same face and braided hair of yarn on the lower right side of the skirt. On the floor she had placed the shoes she wanted me to wear. Black patent-leather loafers she had also brought from the Philippines that looked like comfort shoes made for the elderly.

I looked over to my closet where the simple blue jeans and white T-shirt I had originally laid out were now folded and put away.

My heart sank. I realized my battle with Grandma Fausta had expanded the boundaries of Kiamba and now included La Union. My battle was now with the Oracles as a group, and I had no idea how great their powers were now that they were together.

I started with Grandpa Paterno.

"Please," I begged. "I don't want to wear this to school!"

"But your grandma brought this for you from the Philippines. You will hurt her feelings, Neneng," he said. "Nothing is wrong with these clothes. You will be the most beautiful girl at school." He held the absurd blouse against my shoulders and I knocked it to the ground.

Even Grandpa Paterno's soothing words couldn't help me today. He looked at me in shock and placed his hand on my shoulder. "Don't be like that, Neneng," he said. "Your grandma is just trying to help you."

I put the clothes on after he left the room and began to cry. I cried when I looked in the mirror and saw how ridiculous I looked. But then I cried even more when I realized how much less independence I had now that all of them were here.

Before Grandma Fausta arrived—before any of them arrived—I picked out my own clothes, made my own food, created my own companions. I didn't need them here.

By the time I went downstairs, my nose was running and my eyes were red and puffy. Grandma Patricia put her hands together and exclaimed how wonderful I looked.

"You look like a teenager now!" she said, as if she didn't notice that I had been crying.

"Don't forget your lunch!" Grandma Fausta yelled from the kitchen. She walked over and handed me the brown bag, neatly folded along the top. As I turned to thank her and say good-bye, I was hit by a strong and pungent odor. I continued sniffing, trying to place the familiar scent.

"Are you cooking something?" I asked Grandma Fausta. "I cooked *dinendeng* and rice," she answered. "I put them in your bag for lunch."

I wondered at that moment, with all the religion in our house, if God could hear me begging for mercy.

Not only was I being sent off to school dressed like an overgrown ragdoll, I was also going to be carrying a bag filled with fermented fish. While everyone else would be dining on pizza and sandwiches in the cafeteria, I would be lifting the lid of my Tupperware, unleashing a stench that only the grandchild of four insane Filipino immigrants could possibly understand.

I felt the moisture return to my eyes as I stood there at our entryway. Three steps forward and I would be out the door, on my way to the next stage of my life. But it wasn't that simple at all. My grandfathers were poised to escort me, and I felt more like I was going back in time rather than stepping forward.

All four of them stood there surrounding me, looking proud and emotional. They each had woken up extra early that morning to help prepare me for this day. But what they had prepared me for wasn't the first day of middle school. Instead, it was the first day of school in another country, where children dressed differently and ate differently; they had prepared me for something that was happening thousands of miles away, and I couldn't bring myself to explain that to them.

"This is America," I wanted to say. But I didn't have the heart.

So for that day and for days to come, I left the house as if I were going to school in the Philippines. The other students would call me a "FOB" (fresh off the boat), assuming that I had just come to America. I couldn't explain that it wasn't me but my grandparents who had just come. I continued to wear their clothes and eat their food so that the last bit of the country they left behind would not be taken away from them.

Despite my appearance, one boy—Danny Martin—formed a crush on me and followed me home from school one day. I walked quickly, looking over my shoulder at him and feeling a flush come to my cheeks. My stomach felt woozy, in a way that I had never felt before. His hair was blond and disheveled, his eyes were pale blue.

That day he was wearing worn Levi's, a red and blue striped shirt, and white sneakers—the picture of an all-American boy.

I looked forward, feeling my heart beat against my textbooks.

Before I knew it I was home. I didn't know what to do—turn and talk to him or run inside the house. I heard his footsteps stop as soon as mine did, and I knew he was merely steps away from me.

"Sshhtt!" I heard the universal Filipino call, a sound like air being let out of a tire.

I looked toward our front yard and saw Grandpa Sunday coming from the side of the house holding a hoe. I knew he had been working on his garden.

A surge of panic came over me as I saw him look at me and then at Danny.

"You!" Grandpa yelled. "Go away!"

Suddenly, Grandpa was running toward him with the hoe and Danny was racing down the street. All I saw was a flash of red and blue, and then the back of my grandfather with both arms raised holding the garden tool.

I burst into tears and ran into the house. "I hate you!" I screamed. "I hate all of you!" I buried my head in my pillow, filled with rage and mortification. That was the last time Danny Martin ever followed me home.

· · ·

You're like sure.

Make us proud, Neneng.

I happy. I America.

Don't ever forget where you came from.

Their words rang in my mind like a mantra, a chant, a curse.

I spent my years in middle school symbolically stuck between two generations and customs, and I hated and resented my grandparents for it. More than anything, I wished that I didn't have to be raised by four people whose lives were so different from my own.

I didn't think there was anything more the Oracles could do that would humiliate and infuriate me further—but I under-estimated them. I had forgotten that their sole purpose in coming to this country was to beat down my American will until I became one of them.

The Top 10 countdown was on the local radio station, and I had been listening to it in my room as I fashioned my very own "slam book." In it I wrote questions such as "Who was your first crush?" "Who's your favorite singer?" "Who would you most like to be?" Every It Girl had one at school, passing their books around for others to sign, so I decided it was my time to be It.

But like every moment of escapism I created, it was momentary, and rudely interrupted by the Oracles.

"Are you here?" I heard Grandma Patricia ask as she let herself into my room. I grunted, which was my way of saying, "What the hell do you want now, woman?"

She was beaming, as if she couldn't wait to tell me something. In one hand she was holding a long, beige linen dress with ruffles along the bottom. In the other hand she held a cheesy rhinestone tiara.

"You are going to wear this to the parade!" she shrieked.

I didn't know what parade she was talking about, only that the dress looked hideous to me, and that there was no way that tiara was going on my head.

"Yes! The Filipino lady down the street told me that her granddaughter is going to be Reina Elena in the traditional Filipino beauty parade of princesses, and I told her you could be Reina Sentenciada.

I stared at her as if she were speaking in tongues. I had no idea what she meant, but I knew it was bad.

It turned out that the Filipino lady down the street had never said that her granddaughter was going to be in a parade. This was all Grandma Fausta's idea. Because it was May, she and Grandma Patricia were discussing the Filipino tradition called "Santacruzan." Every May, this historical and religious beauty pageant of sorts was held in Philippine towns and cities to commemorate the discovery of the Holy Cross by Queen Helena (Reina Elena), the mother of Constantine the Great. During the colorful parade, different women dressed in different costumes, each religiously symbolic.

Grandma Patricia suggested how wonderful it would be to bring this tradition to the streets of Vallejo, where people could admire the beauty of their granddaughters. I'm not sure how, but the other Filipino woman in the neighborhood agreed to it, but only if her granddaughter could be Reina Elena, the queen of the parade.

Grandma Patricia settled for me being Reina Sentenciada,

the symbol of the wrongly convicted, whose hands were tied by a rope during the whole procession and who was accompanied by two Roman soldiers. That day, Grandma Patricia had asked my mom to take her shopping so she could find my dress. Afterward they had gone to a pawn shop downtown and found my tiara.

The idea was bad enough since I had no say in the matter, but far worse was the fact that nobody in our neighborhood knew what the Santacruzan was about, or why I and three other girls were dressed up and walking in the middle of the street. Our neighbors on the left side were German, and on the right they were just an all-American white mix. Across the street was a black family, and next to them was another white household. Of course, that didn't matter to Grandma Patricia.

I put the dress on and stared at myself in the mirror with the awful tiara on my head. "Pictures!" yelled Grandma Patricia from the bottom of the stairs. "Come to the front yard so I may take your picture."

I stood on our lawn, cringing every time I heard a car coming down the street. The Oracles stood in front of me, reliving their May fiesta days in the Philippines.

"Good Lord," I thought. "How will I ever outlive the psychological damage this is sure to have on me?"

"Smile!" they each said. But I crossed my arms and growled at the camera. I was tempted to lift my middle finger and flip them all off. They wouldn't have known what it meant anyway.

I walked up and down the street without saying a word to my "Roman soldiers," two scrawny Filipino boys from the neighborhood whom Grandma Patricia had managed to recruit. The Oracles followed along the sidewalk, snapping pictures as if it were some great spectacle. Cars honked at us in anger, neighbors tilted their heads in confusion.

Afterward, I locked my bedroom door, broke the tiara in half, and returned to my slam book, as if the whole thing had never happened.

• • •

My friends told me about it, but I still didn't expect it. I had once seen an illustrated book on my mom's dresser, as if she were planning to talk to me about it, but she never did; she had been acting strangely lately, barely talking and always in her room.

I had just come home after the long walk from school. That day was especially rough. We were in the middle of a heat wave and the sun was burning down on me as I walked up the steep hill that led to our street. When I finally got home, I ran to the bathroom.

I saw the spot of red on the toilet seat and I knew that I had begun my period. My grandpas were outside in the yard and the grandmas were going about their chores in the house. I didn't know if I should wait to tell my mom, or if I should tell my grandmothers.

It was three-thirty in the afternoon and Mom had stayed home from work. I walked quietly upstairs and knocked on her bedroom door, but there was no answer. I cracked the door open to a pitch-black room. Her curtains were drawn and she was under the covers, sleeping. I thought it was strange that she was buried under layers of blankets given the unbearable heat.

I stepped back and shut the door quietly. When I turned around, I was startled to find Grandma Patricia standing behind me holding a stack of freshly folded towels. I gave out a little yell and put my left hand on my heart.

"You should not disturb your mom," she said. "I do not think she feels well."

"But I got my period," I blurted out. "I don't know what to do now."

Suddenly, her serious face became even more serious. "Ay," she whispered. "You are a woman now. You have to be very careful, Neneng."

She pulled me by the arm and led me downstairs into her room and sat me on her bed. I figured this might be "the talk" and I tried hard not to laugh.

Whatever she had to say would not come as a shock to me. My best friend, Sheryl, whom I had met at one of my dad's office parties, had long ago told me about the dynamics of deflowering.

At eight years old, Sheryl was educated in areas that many children that age were not. One day at a family gathering, she told me that her fourteen-year-old cousin was pregnant.

"It's not her fault," I said. "People don't know when they're going to be pregnant."

She looked at me in shock. "What do you mean?" she asked. "She had sex. That's why she's pregnant."

I didn't know what she meant, and she proceeded to explain it to me, using my Barbie and Ken dolls as props. So I was prepared for Grandma Patricia's talk.

She pulled up a chair in front of me and slowly sat down. She reached out and held both of my hands. I knew she would say something that I would always remember and cherish when I got older. These are the words that young women take with them and hold in their hearts as they make their way through womanhood, I thought. I took a deep breath and held her stare.

"Neneng," she started, and then paused. "You should not take showers or baths when you are menstruating. You will get a stomachache if you do that," she said. I had never heard that before, but I figured she must know what she was talking about.

I nodded and waited for Phase Two of our talk—sex.

"And do not ever go to a motel room with a man. That is how women get pregnant. Oh, and do not wear a bra when you are home, it will give you cancer."

And with that, she got up and left the room. That was my talk, and just as I had predicted, I never forgot her words.

When my mom awoke, I shared my news with her. I had expected her to offer more advice than what Grandma Patricia had left me with, but she gave me a weak smile and uttered a few words that I couldn't hear. I was preoccupied by her appearance. She looked disoriented and weak.

"What's wrong, Mom?" I asked.

"I haven't been feeling good." she said.

Though I was worried, I knew she would get all the rest and help she needed with the Oracles around.

Every morning before I left for school, Grandma Fausta was in the kitchen, already preparing vegetables for our dinner. My brother was always with her. Grandma Patricia took care of Mom's laundry, collecting the soiled garments from her room and returning them once they were cleaned and folded. She even cleaned around her vanity, wiping down the counters and mirrors until they sparkled. And every morning, without fail, Grandma Patricia took my mom a cup of coffee. Mom would tell me later that Grandma stood there watching until she was done with the whole cup.

• • •

When I got older, I often thought about middle school and how confusing and frightening it all was. This was the most difficult time for me to come to terms with my grandparents and the roles they each played in my life. While it was common for a teenager to feel as if nobody understood or cared, my upbringing was highly unusual. No counselor, teacher, or friend at school could possibly understand what it felt like to be raised by all of their grandparents—especially *my* grandparents—in one home.

I began slowly pulling away from each of them, talking less and concentrating on MTV more. I stopped taking piano lessons, preferring to crank up the angry vocals of Billy Idol when I craved music.

Sometimes I would hear Grandpa Paterno strumming his guitar in their room, or Grandma Fausta singing her lonely tune. The sounds were faint and pleading, as if reaching out for me to come back. But I pretended not to hear.

There were other distractions in my life. I started having crushes on boys. I began making more friends once I started choosing my own outfits. I began wearing light eyeliner and tinted lip gloss, and I teased my hair, despite my grandmothers' objections.

"You look like a peacock!" they said when I teased my bangs up high and fanned them out like Cyndi Lauper's.

I couldn't balance my new social life with my grandparents' old lives. I felt as if they expected me to bear the burden of their struggles and hardships in the Philippines, and that the more I indulged in fashion, friends, and boys, the more I was betraying the sacrifices they had made.

I was overwhelmed with feelings of outrage, rebellion, resentment, and joy. I needed my mom to listen and comfort me, but it was during my middle school years that she had become invisible.

She was home more often than not, and yet it was as if she was never there. Sometimes she went to work, only to come home in the middle of the day. I watched her climb the stairs and listened to her door shut like a heavy iron gate behind her. I pictured her drawing the curtains and melting away in the cold darkness.

I didn't understand what was happening. She and my dad returned from the hospital saying that the doctor couldn't find anything wrong. But I saw her eyes, lost and vacant; her body, thin and frail. And I knew, in my bones and in my soul, that they were mistaken. There was something very wrong with my mom.

• • •

It was my fourteenth birthday, and my friend Mellie invited me to the movies. My parents weren't home and the Oracles had been going about their daily routines. "I'm going now!" I yelled, expecting them to protest.

"Okay, have fun. Be a good girl there," Grandma Fausta answered from the kitchen.

"Yes, say thank you to Mellie's mom for driving you to the

movies," added Grandma Patricia, in the living room folding clothes.

I headed for the door, confused by the lack of opposition.

Grandpa Sunday was watering plants in the front yard while Grandpa Paterno was bent down pulling weeds. "I'm going now!" I yelled to them, irritated that nobody seemed to care it was my birthday.

Grandpa Sunday flashed me his classic smile, nodding his head and waving good-bye.

"Okay, Neneng. Be good," said Grandpa Paterno.

I stomped on the pavement, all the way to Mellie's house five blocks away. I was furious at everyone.

"If it was my brother's birthday, they would have at least cooked something!" I complained to my friend. "Grandma Fausta would have made a cake for him, I bet!"

"Oh, never mind. Let's just have fun and forget it," she said.

After the movie, Mellie said she would come back home with me so I wouldn't feel alone on my birthday. By now it was dusk and the November air was cold and dry. I looked at the sinking sun, casting a lavender haze across the sky.

Dusk was always my favorite time, still and majestic, when sins could be forgiven and a new beginning was just beyond the pastel horizon. "I guess this birthday wasn't so bad," I said, turning to Mellie.

"You see, I told you," she said, hugging my arm.

When we got to my house, there were no signs of anyone home. I stepped over the stream of water trickling along the sidewalk, carrying with it the extra water from our saturated lawn. I couldn't imagine where everyone had gone.

"Don't close the door yet," I told Mellie. The house was dark except for the stream of light in the entryway coming from the streetlamp. I flipped on the switch in the kitchen and fell to the floor when a house of faceless, nameless people yelled a collective "SURPRISE!"

I turned to look at Mellie, who was laughing at the door. "We got you!" she yelled.

I looked around the kitchen, the family room, all along the stairway and saw friends from school, cousins, aunts, uncles, and neighbors.

And there, in front of a table covered with the most beautiful, colorful Filipino dishes and the biggest birthday cake I had ever seen, were my four grandparents, my mom, my dad, and my brother, all wearing birthday hats.

"You see?" Grandma Patricia said, placing both her hands over her heart. "You see how we all love you?"

And once again, the music began to play.

Above: My parents took me to the Philippines in 1973, when I was four years old. Here, Grandpa Sunday gives me and my cousins a tour of his farmland in Kiamba from atop a water buffalo. I am at the back.

Right: Grandma Fausta's first day in America, posing with my father in our kitchen, where she spent countless hours snapping green beans.

Left: Grandma Fausta seldom smiled, but when she did she was often with my baby brother, Christopher.

Right: This is one of two photos of my cousin Riza that Grandma Fausta had on her dresser. She often bragged that Riza was crowned the Queen of Kiamba and was Grandpa Sunday's favorite. I stole the photo out of jealousy.

Left: My first trip to Disneyland, cut short by Grandma Fausta's ailing hip.

Above: One of my first photos taken with Grandma Fausta. I'm eight years old here, wearing a dress chosen by her.

Below: My first Christmas after Grandpa Paterno arrived in America in 1979; I had just turned ten. I protested wearing this dress, which Grandma Fausta chose for me.

Above: In 1981, Grandpa Sunday used his carpentry skills to build this patio in our backyard in Vallejo, California.

Right: Grandma Patricia and Grandma Fausta before Sunday Mass.

Above: Despite my visible anger, the Oracles snapped this photo of me just before forcing me to march up and down our street for a traditional Filipino "parade."

Left: My senior photo, taken in 1987.

Above: The last time my grandparents were all together in America was at my wedding, on November 17, 1990. Grandma Patricia is standing to the left of my father, who is next to me. Next to her is Grandma Fausta. Directly behind them are Grandpa Paterno and Grandpa Sunday.

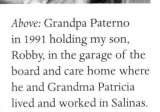

Above: Grandpa Paterno in 1991 holding my son, Robby, in the garage of the board and care home where he and Grandma Patricia lived and worked in Salinas.

Left: Grandma Patricia and Grandpa Paterno at a party thrown for them in the Philippines when they returned home for good.

Above: The church at Grandpa Sunday's funeral in the small town of Kiamba was filled with hundreds of people who came to say good-bye.

Below: My uncles and cousins transfer Grandpa Sunday's coffin from the home he shared with Grandma Fausta to a hearse. Seconds earlier, a live chicken was thrown under the coffin and sacrificed as part of an old provincial ritual.

Above: Before re-entering Grandma Fausta's home after the funeral, guests were forced to ward the spirits away by washing their hair with warm vinegar and burnt herbs.

Below: My brother, Christopher, me, and my mom with Grandma Fausta in front of Grandpa Sunday's coffin.

Chapter Eight

Old Wounds

Grandpa Paterno was having a difficult time finding work. He had heard from one of my dad's friends that there were seasonal jobs on the farms in Salinas, two and a half hours from our house. There, he could harvest and package asparagus, lettuce, and broccoli. During the week, Grandpa Paterno could stay in the sleeping quarters set up for migrant workers, then come home on the weekends.

Both he and Grandma Patricia agreed it was the best thing for him to do. Their plan had always been to come to America, make enough money to retire, then return to the Philippines and live a comfortable life on Grandpa Paterno's pension.

But both were reluctant to make the decision. They had already been separated for two years when Grandpa Paterno came to America. It seemed that in their quest for a better life, they were often sacrificing each other.

Dad assured them that we would drive to Salinas every Saturday to pick him up. "Don't worry," he said. "You'll see each other every weekend."

Grandma Patricia had been crying. It was the night before Grandpa Paterno's departure and he was packing a week's worth of clothes into his canvas duffle bag. I sat on the floor of their bedroom watching him fold his white cotton undershirts, flannel long-sleeves, and pairs of sweatpants and worn denims. Grandma Patricia counted five handkerchiefs out of his drawer and tucked them away neatly into the side pocket of his bag, saving an extra one for herself to wipe her tears.

Grandma Patricia sat at the foot of the bed, silently weeping. I saw Grandpa Paterno move the zipper of his bag slowly along its teeth, careful not to create the zipping sound that would have indicated he was ready to go. I failed to understand what all the melodrama was about. "It's not like he's going to the Philippines. You're going to see him every weekend," I said to Grandma Patricia.

"Don't you know I cannot live without your grandpa?" she said, looking at me through eyes filled with tears and heartbreak. "He is like my statue of the Santo Niño. He watches over me and protects me."

The next morning, Dad woke us all up at five so we could hit the road early. On the farm, Grandpa Paterno said, they would be waking up at four or five every morning to start work. Though Dad tried to keep the mood light during the drive, I could feel the weight of Grandma Patricia's sorrow. Grandpa held her hand tightly.

My dad pulled up alongside a one-story beige building. The structure was old, with cracked paint and streams of dirt running from its rain gutters. Along the side there were a series of small rectangle windows with bottles of shampoo and other toiletries lined along the sills. Grandpa Paterno grabbed his duffle bag from the van and looked at the piece of paper on which he had written down the address of where he would be staying. "This is the right place," he said, turning to all of us.

He knocked on the door and was greeted by a Hispanic man with a large straw hat. *"Hola,"* Grandpa said. "I am Paterno. I will be working here."

Through the crack I could see a small sink piled up with dirty dishes and a row of narrow beds covered with brown wool blankets. I pictured Grandpa Paterno lying awake in one of them, staring at the ceiling, surrounded by sleeping strangers, and wondering if this was the America he had long dreamed of.

While Grandpa Paterno was away during the week, Grandma Patricia continued her regular chores at home. But she had grown quieter and her demeanor more sullen. She walked around the house carrying the laundry basket low by her knees, hunching her back and drooping her shoulders as if it was filled with hardened cement.

After a while, her sorrow had evolved to bitterness. "Your mom doesn't know how to arrange her clothes!" she said one day. I had walked into my parents' room looking for a brush and found her sitting on the carpet in front of my mom's closet next to a heaping pile of clothes. She had cleared the shelves and taken everything off the hangers and thrown it on the floor so she could re-fold and re-hang everything—her way.

I stood in amazement, looking back and forth between my grandmother, the empty closet, and the doorway. I was afraid that at any moment my mom would walk in and bear witness to Grandma Patricia's random act of madness.

"What are you doing?" I asked. Her behavior frightened me, and yet I stood defiant, as if the clothes were each pieces of my mother and Grandma Patricia was ripping her apart.

"All this money! Your dad makes money and your mom spends it on all these clothes. Now she has so many she can't even arrange them nicely in her closet," she said. She went on talking while she threw the clothes about angrily, not once turning to look at me.

I was standing by the window, which overlooked the street and a patch of our front yard to the left. I caught a glimpse of Grandma Fausta and Grandpa Sunday watering plants and I wondered what they would say if they could hear what their *abalayan* was saying about their daughter.

• • •

Months had passed since my mom first began feeling ill. She had taken numerous tests—an MRI, blood tests—and tried various treatments—acupuncture, psychotherapy, exercise—but no doctor could find anything wrong, and no treatment seemed to help.

She complained constantly about shooting pains in her neck and down the middle of her back. She often felt weak and began to perspire, complaining that she felt cold and dizzy. At first, her doctors said she was experiencing anxiety attacks, but they had no explanation for her physical pains. After a while, she decided to quit work.

Dad had been working part-time as a realtor while keeping his job at Blue Cross. During the height of the real estate boom in the eighties, he decided to get a broker's license and open his own business along with my mom. Because her health was so unpredictable, working for themselves was the perfect answer for both of them.

During the ribbon-cutting ceremony of my parents' new office, the Oracles stood alongside each other, proud of their children's accomplishment. A photographer from the local paper showed up to capture the scene for the Business section. "This is my son's office," Grandma Patricia told him. Grandma Fausta kept her smile, although I swore I saw her flinch.

My parents' modest success was timed with Grandpa Paterno's move to Salinas. While Grandma Patricia was thrilled for my father, she was envious and resentful of my mom, whose husband didn't have to leave her side to earn money.

Perhaps it was because I bore her name that Grandma Patricia felt she could remove her mask in front of me. In front of everyone else, she was a helpful, loving mother-in-law, but when we were alone, I felt the heaviness in her heart, and I saw a decades-old anger in her eyes.

I never mentioned Grandma Patricia's true feelings to anyone in the house. Mom and Dad had just started the business and Grandma Fausta and Grandpa Sunday seemed happier than ever now that more of their children had come to America. My Aunt Evangeline, the youngest of my mom's five sisters, had just moved into a house two blocks away from ours with her husband and two kids, and Uncle Jun, born Domingo Junior, the second youngest of my mom's five brothers, had moved in three blocks away with his wife and two sons. Grandma Fausta and Grandpa Sunday walked from one house to the next, babysitting my cousins, cooking and eating with each family. They felt like their village in the Philippines had been recreated.

Mom's spirits were lifted with her siblings nearby. She had comfort and support, but she would often tell me that what she craved most was a sense of peace.

I was in front of the mirror spraying Sun-In all over my hair when I heard my mom calling me from her room. The formula promised to bring out my natural highlights and brighten the color of my hair. I was eager to reinvent myself without my grandparents noticing; I'd read on the label that the change would occur gradually with more exposure to the sun.

I wrapped my hair up in a towel and walked over to my mom, who was standing in front of her bed looking into a compact mirror.

"Do you want to come to a prayer meeting with me?" she asked.

"For what?" I replied.

"There's a lady who's sick and the Santo Niño Lady is going to pray over her," she answered plainly, as if she were simply talking about the weather.

I didn't know what the "Santo Niño Lady" was, and I felt I had sacrificed enough of my childhood learning about the supernatural. "I think I'll stay home," I said, "but have loads of fun." At fourteen, I had mastered the art of sarcasm.

The morning mist and chill had given way to a crystal blue sky that afternoon. After Mom left for her prayer meeting, I called Mellie to come over so we could give each other perms with the cheap box sets we bought at the drugstore.

I created a mock beautician's station in the upstairs bathroom with glasses and cups holding the various instruments, combs, brushes, clips. I set Grandpa Sunday's boombox on the shelf behind us and cranked up the volume to Pat Benatar's "Love Is a

Battlefield."

Mellie and I screamed out the lyrics, holding the hairbrushes to our mouths. *We are young, heartache to heartache we stand. No promises, no demands. Love is a battlefield.* We took turns listing off the cutest guys at school as we rolled each other's hair and screeched with laughter.

"Stop it!" Grandma Patricia yelled up the stairs. "Are you young ladies or wild beasts?"

Mellie and I turned and looked at each other and broke out into hysterical laughter. "We're beasts!" I yelled back. She and Grandma Fausta stormed upstairs to scold us, but it was no use. Pat Benatar had fueled us with enough eighties-inspired girl power to rival their Old World cynicism. The grandmothers looked at us in shock as we stood before them, two girls who could have easily been them had they not been born in another time and place.

"Like sure!" Grandma Fausta said in disgust, taking Grandma Patricia's arm as they both headed back downstairs. Mellie and I were quiet for a while, knowing that we had won the standoff. Pat continued to croon in the background, her words inspiring and elevating us even more.

We are strong, no one can tell us we're wrong. Searching our hearts for so long, both of us knowing, love is a battlefield.

Mom came home long after dinner later that night. Mellie and I were listening to the radio in my bedroom, lying on our stomachs and flipping through *Teen Beat* magazines on the floor when we heard the garage door open and close.

"My parents are finally home," I told Mellie. Our heads were topped with freshly permed hair, tight curls framing our faces. We had both left the formula on too long. Combined with the Sun-In that I had already been using, my hair had turned a shocking orange. "I look like an Asian Orphan Annie," I said to Mellie, looking in the mirror. Even at the height of punk, I looked slightly ridiculous.

We were reading an article on Molly Ringwald when Mellie and

I heard something coming from Grandma Patricia and Grandpa Paterno's room below us. At first there were muffled sounds, as if numerous people were talking at once. Then the murmurs stopped and a low, continuous sound ensued.

"Is someone singing?" Mellie asked.

We both turned our heads to the side, literally putting our ears to the ground. I wondered if Grandma was saying one of her chants or prayers again. The sound was dark and throaty, like the prayer Catholic priests sing during mass while holding up the body of Christ and snapping it in two.

I heard Mom's voice, weak and frightened, followed by crying. I grew nervous. The sounds went on for another hour—murmurs, sobbing, elevated voices, then silence—before we heard a door open and close. Mellie and I sat up and looked at my door, wondering if we should venture outside or stay protected in my room. I turned the radio back on, pretending my family didn't exist and that I was a normal American girl having a silly time with my best friend.

"Aren't you going to see what happened?" Mellie asked.

But I knew, by my racing heart and the chill in my bones, that whatever had happened downstairs was something more than trouble with the in-laws. It was going to change everything.

• • •

The jarring buzz from my alarm clock woke me at seven-thirty the next morning. As usual, I pressed the snooze button, slept for ten more minutes, then dragged myself into the bathroom.

My sleepy eyes widened in shock when I looked in the mirror and saw that the tight curls I had the night before had morphed into an afro. I began panicking, dousing my head with water and hair gel, then pulling my hair back in a ponytail. I threw on my clothes for school—a denim miniskirt with an oversized top cinched at the waist with a big belt.

I headed downstairs and into the kitchen, expecting to see

Grandma Fausta preparing my breakfast like she did every morning. Instead, I found my mom hunched over the sink with Grandma Patricia next to her. I moved closer and saw that my mom was vomiting.

Grandma's hand was on my mom's back, not rubbing it in a comforting way but simply placed on it. "What's wrong?" I said, remembering the sounds I'd heard the night before. My mom looked up and Grandma turned toward me. Both sets of eyes were red and puffy. Then Grandpa Paterno came out of the room.

"Why are you here?" I asked. "Why aren't you in Salinas?"

Nobody answered me as I stood there completely confused. "What's happening?" I asked, looking at each of them.

"Your mom doesn't feel good," said Grandpa Paterno.

"We will be leaving you," Grandma Patricia jumped in, now beginning to cry. "We have to leave you, Neneng. When you come home from school, we will no longer be here."

My mom had stopped vomiting, and her back was turned to me now.

Grandma Patricia walked over to me, grabbing me tightly. "We love you, we love you," she kept repeating as she wept on my shoulder. "Always be good. I cannot watch you now that we must leave you."

I didn't understand what was happening. I only knew that whatever it was that she was feeling, I could feel it too. I began to cry, releasing a deep, sorrowful, soulful sound that gave me the chills and made the hairs on my arm stand. It was a sound brought over from another place and time, where people longed and suffered and worshipped and rejoiced.

It was all of those things in one powerful expression, but this time it was coming from me.

Chapter Nine

Revelations

Mom didn't know the sick woman she would be praying for at the meeting, but she had heard about the Santo Niño Lady who channeled spirits and was said to have healing powers. People believed her gift was from the Baby Jesus since a child's voice would emerge from her mouth when she began channeling.

My mom had not told anyone that she had been suffering the past few months. She went to the prayer meeting partially out of curiosity, wondering if this mysterious healer could find something for her that doctors could not: a cause and a cure for her pain.

She was a bit nervous when she rang the doorbell. Mom had never met a faith healer before and she didn't know what to expect. She was relieved when her friend Monica opened the door and greeted her with a hug and kisses on both cheeks. They were chatting in the entryway when my mom felt a slight touch on her arm. She turned and saw an old lady with concern in her eyes staring back at her.

"Who is in your house?" the Santo Niño Lady asked my mom. "Someone is playing with your body."

My mom felt faint, holding on to the banister. "My mother-in-law lives with us," she whispered.

"She is doing something to you," the woman answered. "Have you not been sick?"

My mom could not drive home after the meeting. Her head
was spinning and her heart was racing. She had never believed
in faith healers or people who claimed to channel spirits before,
but she couldn't explain how this woman knew that she had
been sick. Nor could she explain why the first question the old
woman asked was who was in her house.

Mom wondered if it could be true. If Grandma's years of
superstition and black magic were powerful enough to leave
the jungles and fields of the Philippines and emerge in the tract
homes and asphalt streets of her American life.

She called my dad and waited outside on the cool steps of
the porch. In her mind, she went over everyday scenes: the cups
of coffee every morning that Grandma watched her drink, the
clothes she couldn't find every time Grandma did her laundry,
the hair missing from her brushes every time Grandma cleaned
her vanity.

When my dad arrived, she collapsed in his arms. She didn't
know how to tell him that his mother had to leave. How could
she tell him what she couldn't understand herself?

"We have to get *Tatang*," she said. "Tatang" was what Dad
called Grandpa Paterno.

And so they drove to Salinas. My mom didn't say a word on
the way there, and my dad didn't ask. He held her hand tightly
during the drive, and when they came back with Grandpa
Paterno, they went straight into the bedroom below mine and
let my mother talk.

She couldn't understand the words she was saying. She often
told me years later that it wasn't her talking in the room, it was
the Santo Niño Lady. Grandma Patricia cried as Mom spoke,
never admitting or denying anything, only weeping.

Grandpa Paterno stayed silent, comforting Grandma, then
turning to my mom. "We would never hurt you, but we will go
if that will make it better," he said.

Mom's heart ached for Grandpa Paterno. No matter what
Grandma may have done, he was the kindest, most patient man
she had ever known. And yet she had no choice; one would

never leave the barrel without the other.

The next morning, Mom was in the kitchen when Grandma Patricia came up behind her and placed her hand firmly on her back.

"And then it was as if all those months of suffering just came out," she finally told me when I was in high school. "I began to vomit, like your grandma allowed the evil spirits to leave my body."

The Two Pats moved out that day, to Salinas where they both found themselves surrounded by stretches of farmland once more.

Mom's illness ended the day they moved out.

After a while, my mom emerged from the cocoon she had turned her bedroom into. Now, when she came home from work she went to the kitchen and began cooking instead of retreating to her bed. I didn't know what had caused the change, and inside I felt it was best I didn't ask. My first middle school dance was coming up and all I wanted to do was distance myself from all the strangeness and secrecy.

I didn't know if anyone would ask me to the dance, but I longed to go. For once, I wanted to just be an average girl at an ordinary dance in a smelly gym. "Please, God," I sat up in bed and prayed. "Please let a boy ask me to the dance."

One weekend, my mom suggested I visit my friend Sheryl in Dublin, which was about forty-five minutes from where we lived. I didn't ask why, though I assumed, with both the Pats now gone, she thought it was best for me to get away. I packed two days' worth of clothes and jumped into the car. Though we stayed in touch over the phone and through letters, I really hadn't seen Sheryl since I'd started middle school. Now we were both fifteen and I couldn't wait to catch up.

We screamed and hugged each other when I got there. I kissed my mom and told her to take her time picking me up on Sunday. I hadn't realized how much the problems between my mom and Grandma Patricia had weighed me down. Here, in my friend's house, miles away from our home, I felt an incredible sense of freedom and relief. I wished I could move in with her, where there were no grandparents, and no mysteries.

We stayed up the whole night talking. Sheryl had a boyfriend named Mark, she told me, and I was filled with envy. "We can ride my bike to the park tomorrow and meet him there," she said. I couldn't wait.

The next morning, I put on my favorite pair of blue jeans and a black canvas jacket. I looked at myself in the mirror, teasing my front bangs out and clipping my hair on both sides. Even though I was meeting Sheryl's boyfriend, I was just excited that I was meeting a boy at all. I imagined that it was *my* boyfriend I was going to see and that it was our special park we were meeting at.

I rode on the back of Sheryl's bike, holding on to the metal bar behind me. My heart was racing and my palms had begun to perspire. The bangs that I had fluffed up were now getting an extra boost from the wind. By the time we got there, I looked like a peacock in full bloom.

"There he is," she said, pointing to a short, stocky guy standing by the swings. His hair was long in the back, forming a narrow V shape. He was wearing baggy pants, which every cool Asian guy seemed to wear in those days, and a black leather jacket. She set the bike down and ran to him, giving him a huge hug and kiss on the cheek. I stared shamelessly, wishing I was part of the couple and not the outsider.

"This is my cousin Pati," she said to him. We weren't technically cousins, but we always told people we were. He nodded his head in a way that said "I'm too cool to say hi." So I nodded my head back in a way that said "I'm not sure what I'm doing."

They held hands and began to walk away from the park. I stood there, wondering if I was supposed to follow or just wait. Sheryl looked back and waved me over. "Come on!" she yelled. "We're going to his house."

I wasn't sure what my grandparents would say about me going to a boy's house. All Grandma Patricia warned me about was going to a motel room; she never said anything about a house. I pretended that reasoning made it okay, though I knew they would have made me pray the rosary three times if they knew what I was doing.

The house was empty when we got there. I sat on a plastic-covered couch and looked away as they kissed each other in front of me. Then, before I knew it, they disappeared. I didn't know where they went, so I sat there waiting, and waiting. An hour later, I began to get angry. I walked down the hall but every door was closed and I was scared to open any of them. I began coughing loudly to remind her that I was still waiting, but nothing happened.

When the doorbell rang I thought they would surely emerge from whatever it was that they were doing, but there was still no sign of them. I opened the door, even though I had no idea whose house I was in. There, standing on the porch, was the cutest guy I had ever seen. His eyes were dark and friendly, his skin a light mocha. I stood there melting, not knowing what to say.

"Is Mark here?" he asked.

"Yeah, but I don't know where he is exactly," I said.

"Who are you?" he asked, confused by my answer.

"I'm Sheryl's friend, Pati," I said, still staring.

"Oh!" he said. "I'm Dave."

He walked through the door and got comfortable on the couch. "So that means Sheryl's here, right?" he said with a huge grin. "Don't worry about where they are; they'll be out when they're ready."

I got a funny feeling, as if he was talking dirty. I was like a country bumpkin thrown into the fast lane of normal, hormonal teenage life. I had a lot of catching up to do.

Dave began asking questions about my school and where I lived. He told me he had relatives in Vallejo and that he went to visit them sometimes. "What kinds of things do you do?" he asked.

I didn't know what to say. I didn't want to tell him that in my spare time I washed laundry with my bare hands and hung it out to dry, or that I'd spend hours trying to communicate with my Grandpa Sunday, who spoke barely any English at all. I didn't want to tell him that up until recently all four of my grandparents lived with me and that they were my core social group. I didn't want him to see how pathetic my life was.

"Oh, I do stuff," I answered coyly.

Suddenly, Sheryl and Mark emerged from the room, both of them looking tired and disheveled. My face turned hot. I was ashamed for her and angry that she left me to fend for myself on a plastic-covered couch. I shot her a hard look, hoping it would have the same effect on her that Grandma Fausta's looks had on me.

"Sorry," she said.

But I didn't answer. I felt like calling my grandmothers and telling them what she had done, if only to prove to them that I wasn't such a bad girl after all. Sheryl and I didn't speak the whole night. I wondered if she was having sex and, if so, when she had lost her virginity. And then I wondered if maybe I was the freak, that maybe I had been so sheltered by my grandparents that I had missed out on what all the other kids my age were doing.

All I knew was that I was uncomfortable and I wanted to go home to my grandparents, where everything was pure and good.

A week had gone by since "the incident" in Dublin. I never told anyone about it, nor did I even want to remember it. When Sheryl called, I didn't know what to say to her.

"Umm, I know you're mad at me, but I have something to tell you," she said. I waited for her to continue, not saying a word.

"Dave said his cousin told him there was a dance at your school this week and he wanted to know if he could take you to it."

Suddenly, nothing Sheryl did mattered. I let out a scream and felt a joy that I had never felt before. I was so excited about having a date that I had completely forgotten the most crucial part about going to the dance—asking permission.

"No way," my dad said. We were at the dinner table when I asked and I knew Grandma Fausta was looking at me.

"But it's Sheryl's friend I'm going with and you'll meet him and everything," I begged, knowing that my parents thought Sheryl was an angel.

My dad looked over at my mom. They took a few minutes communicating with their eyes before he finally relented. "Okay, but I will drive you there and you have to be home by nine-thirty," he said. It didn't matter to me what time he said, all I heard was "yes" and that was enough.

Grandma Fausta came with my mom and me to the mall the next day to search for my first dress for my first dance with the first boy I would ever go out with. It was quite an occasion, and one I would have preferred Grandma not be a part of, but even she couldn't dampen my spirits.

I looked at a shiny sleeveless blue dress with ruffles at the bottom. "Oooh!" I exclaimed.

"Hmph!" replied Grandma. "You will look like a hostess." I knew she was referring to the prostitutes in the Philippines, so I kept quiet and rolled my eyes.

"How about this one?" I asked, pointing to a more conservative black dress.

"You'll look like you're going to a funeral," she said.

I was growing tired and frustrated. I realized that, in the end, it would be Grandma Fausta who chose what I would wear to the dance, which meant I might as well have gone in a traditional Filipino dress, a la Imelda Marcos.

"That one," she said, pointing to a gray and black striped dress that hung loose and shapeless on the hanger.

"Ooh, that's nice," my mom said, taking it off the rack.

"Fine," I grunted. "I'll look like a potato sack."

But it didn't matter. That night, on the balcony overlooking an endless stretch of grass, Dave leaned over and gave me my first real kiss. And there was nothing any of the Oracles could do about it.

Just when he pulled me closer, I felt something fall out of my coat pocket and heard it drop on the cement. Dave and I both stopped kissing to see what it was, and there, in the middle of my romantic kiss, was Grandma Fausta's rosary, which she had managed to sneak into my pocket before I left the house.

I was wrong. It didn't matter where I was, who I was kissing, or how I dressed, the Oracles were always with me.

• • •

A small bead of sweat was making its way down my temple, leaving a shimmering snail's trail as it moved along the curve of my jaw. I took the handkerchief Grandma Patricia had left in her room and that I had saved for more than two years, and quickly wiped it before it reached my neck. I had been driving for more than an hour now and the heat was suffocating.

The road ahead looked like ground charcoal, heat rising from it and distorting the images ahead. I turned the radio off, thinking the silence would cool the air.

"You know, sometimes it was so hot on the farm I would sit under a coconut tree for shade. Sometimes I would not wake for three hours," I heard Grandpa Paterno's voice in my head. But I looked around at the dismal landscape on both sides of the freeway—dry, brown hills, ripe for an Indian summer grass fire. No coconut trees, no shade in sight.

I grabbed onto the steering wheel with my left hand while I pulled out the flimsy rectangle sheet that read "Temporary Driver's License" with my right.

I had been waiting to hold that piece of paper since I was eight years old. On days when my grandparents would drone on about the Old Country, I often fantasized about the day I'd become an official driver. I pictured myself pulling out of the driveway—no destination in mind, just anywhere but where they were. With my license, I escaped the smells of their provincial food and headed for the comforts of a classic American fast-food drive-thru. The sounds of my car stereo and the wind blowing through the window drowned out their stories of struggle. Only then, I thought, would I finally be free of the Oracles.

But when that day finally arrived, I called the Two Pats. "I'll be driving to Salinas to see you next week," I told Grandpa Paterno. "Can you tell Grandma to cook me *dinendeng* with okra and bamboo shoots?"

During that first week after I got my license, I had driven Grandma Fausta to every Asian market in town, loading the trunk of my blue Honda hatchback with bags of fish, crabs, taro root, eggplant, cans of coconut milk, sacks of Jasmine long grain rice, and heaps of Chinese long green beans. Grandpa Sunday and I went to various department stores, spending hours in their electronics and music departments as he loaded up with more country cassette tapes. He popped them into my car stereo and began moving his head to the honky-tonk beat and lyrics he didn't understand.

Now I was driving more than two hours to spend the weekend with my other grandparents, whom I had so desperately tried all those years to escape.

I had only seen Grandma Patricia three times since she'd left. Before she moved out, it was as if there was a nervous buzz around the house, like the sounds of different music boxes playing at once—no order, no harmony, just movement and confusion. But after she left, the music stopped. Nobody spoke of what happened. Grandma Fausta and Grandpa Sunday went on with their daily routines, though now they seemed to be incomplete. I wondered what was worse, the noise Grandma Patricia's presence caused those last few months or the silence her departure left behind.

Mom would only tell me that Grandma Patricia was doing something bad to her and that everyone agreed it was best if they moved out.

"But what did she do?" I'd ask.

"You won't understand" was all she would say.

Grandma Fausta was quick to hush me whenever I asked if she knew what had happened that night.

"But do you think she did something bad?" I asked.

"I can not say," she answered. "Only God knows."

I didn't understand for years, even after my mom told me in detail what had happened. I only knew that I missed the music, and I relied on my new car to lead me back to it.

Grandma Patricia was sitting on the porch when I pulled up to the small one-story house. In the garage were four disheveled men sitting at a card table. Grandma Patricia jumped to her feet and ran toward my car in her house slippers, pants, and a lavender turtleneck. Looking at her winter outfit made me perspire even more.

"You're here!" she yelled, throwing her arms around me.

There was a part of me that felt like I was home when I saw her, and yet I felt a little awkward. I wondered if she really had something to do with my mom's illness, and if she did, was I betraying my mom by being there?

"Hi, Grandma" was all I could say as I saw her eyes well up.

"Come," she said, "let us pass through the garage."

The four men looked up at us as we walked toward them. "This is my granddaughter!" Grandma Patricia yelled. "You see? She has come to visit us!"

None of them answered. Two of the men looked confused, while the other two seemed as if they didn't even hear her.

The door coming in from the garage went straight into a small, crowded bedroom with a full-size bed pushed up against a wall. Everything seemed to be stacked to the ceiling—blankets, albums, boxes. "This is where your grandpa and I sleep," she said.

She opened another door, which led to a small kitchen with avocado green Formica counters and a wood table placed in the center of the linoleum floor. "Neneng!" Grandpa Paterno looked up from the rice cooker he was tending to. "Oh, it's so nice to see you here."

Just past the kitchen I could see an old television and two women sitting on a brown couch in front of it. The house smelled like mildew and chicken broth.

"Hi," I called out to them. Both looked up at me, then slowly turned their heads back to face the set.

"Grandpa, who are they? And who are those men in the garage?" I whispered.

"This is a board and care home," he answered. "Some of them are very sick. The others don't even know what is going on around them."

"But you don't belong in a care home," I said.

"We're not one of them, we take care of them," he explained. "This is the only way Grandma and I can have a free room and earn a little money."

I looked around at the small house, the two women, my grandparents' cramped bedroom. I felt guilt and shame and anger. I didn't deserve to drive a new car, and they didn't deserve to live this life. I blamed my parents for sending them away.

I helped Grandpa Paterno set the table for the boarders while Grandma Patricia bathed one of the female patients who was suffering from Alzheimer's.

"Cigarette. Cigarette. Cigarette," said one of the men as he approached me in the kitchen.

"No, Carlos!" Grandpa Paterno yelled with a smile. He walked over to the young man, who looked like he was in his early thirties, and gently held his arm, leading him back into the garage. "No cigarettes today. It's almost time to eat."

"Cigarette. Cigarette," he repeated, placing his fingers to his mouth to show he wanted to smoke.

"He always asks," Grandpa explained to me. "But he doesn't even know how to smoke. He's never smoked here before."

A small yell came from the bathroom. "Get away from me!" the woman's voice cried.

"I am just making you clean," I heard Grandma Patricia say. "Don't you want to be clean so you can sleep well tonight?"

"Don't touch me!" yelled the woman.

I put down the plates I had been holding and ran to my car, passing through the garage and by those same four men, who turned to stare.

I sat in the driver's seat, laid my head on the steering wheel, and began to cry. I wept for my grandparents and the dreams that had evaporated the day they stepped into this house filled with lost souls and broken lives. I wished I could tell them to pack their bags and load them into my car so I could bring them home.

I shut my eyes and continued to cry until I heard a light tapping on my window.

"It's okay, Neneng," Grandpa Paterno said. "We are okay here. They are our family now."

They stayed with their new family for five more years, until they decided it was time to finally go home, to the real family they had left behind years ago.

Chapter Ten

Leaving America

Granda Fausta and Grandpa Sunday kept their room at our house, but they would often stay at my aunt's place just two blocks away to take care of her two young children, Jamelyn and Justin. "Poor cousins," I thought, knowing they would be tortured the way I was.

Grandma Fausta also began babysitting toddlers from around the neighborhood. My mom told the white families to call her "Grandma Faye" so she would sound more American. Every morning, four toddlers in diapers would be dropped off and left in the care of Grandma Faye.

Sometimes Grandma Fausta and Grandpa Sunday would go to Suisun with my Uncle Jun, his wife, Auntie Nelia, and their two small boys, Andrew and Kevin. My grandparents had their own room there as well and would often stay for weeks at a time to take care of the boys.

With a new crop of children to care for, I was free of Grandma Fausta. When I came home from college on the weekends, the house was often empty. My parents were off selling houses, Grandma and Grandpa Pat were miles away in Salinas, my brother spent most of his time at his friend's house down the street, and the other set of Oracles were tending to their new set of grandchildren.

It was during this small window of time that I felt a sense of pure freedom. The house smelled clean and American, no scent of fried fish permeating the carpet and walls, no one comparing me to my saintly cousins in the Philippines. For once, I wasn't afraid of what I would find when I got home.

But now I felt like the last crab in the barrel. While all my other friends had enjoyed their teen years, I was pickled in a jar of anchovy broth. My grandparents had preserved me in their own little cocoon of folklore and old tradition. They had kept me a little girl—*their* little girl—while everyone else had grown up around me. I felt the need to catch up—and fast.

I began drinking beer and smoking cigarettes. I experimented with marijuana, though my first experience was enough to make me kick the habit. One of my roommates had brought some weed from San Diego, "the good, pure shit," she called it. So we passed the little rolled-up bud around as we all sat in a circle on the carpet of our empty apartment.

When it was my turn, I thought of my grandparents and what they would do if they saw me now. For some reason, the thought made me smile. After a while, I wasn't only smiling, I was laughing in slow motion. I mimicked my grandparents one by one, complete with their heavy accents.

"You bad girl using drugs! You go hell!" I said, pointing to my roommates, who were just as wasted as I was at that point.

But then something happened. I felt like my head was slowly falling off. I held my arms out in front of me to catch it, but I couldn't figure out which way it was falling. "You guys," I said with what little energy I could muster. "My head's falling. Help me." My roommates were laughing at me and all I could think of was my grandparents having to identify a headless torso.

That was the last time I used marijuana. I instead focused my attention on another thing I had missed out on—the opposite sex.

It was after a late morning class that I met Ruben. He was sitting next to my friend Jose, whom I had known in high school. I walked over, giving Jose a hug and engaging in casual conversation. "You know Pati?" he asked his friend. Ruben had on a brown leather jacket and a small biking cap. "Nu-uh," he answered. After the introductions, I rushed off, remembering I had to drive Grandpa Sunday to a doctor's appointment by noon.

I didn't think of Ruben again until a week later when I saw Jose at the bookstore.

"So what do you think of my friend?" he asked.

"What friend?"

"Ruben, man. He thinks you're pretty."

Later that day I saw Ruben sitting in the middle of the quad. This time he was wearing stonewashed blue jeans, a button-down shirt, and no hat. His light-brown eyes and fair skin made me think he was Hispanic. Lining his jaw was a five o'clock shadow that would have made even George Michael proud. "Hmmm," I thought. "Not bad."

I walked over and said hi, asking him what class he had just come out of and if he was done for the day. He explained that his car wasn't working and he was waiting for his mom to pick him up. I could tell he was embarrassed to admit that, but I found it kind of cute. I offered to drive him home. He offered to take me out.

Perhaps a wild college party with kegs of beer and loud music wasn't the most romantic of choices, but that was our first date. I asked him to pick me up at my parents' house since I was home for the weekend. I didn't expect Grandma Fausta and Grandpa Sunday to be home too, but they were.

I tried to hide the skintight leggings I was wearing, along with the sheer black top that revealed a small camisole underneath. But just as the doorbell rang, Grandma emerged from her room. She looked at me from head to toe in shock and what seemed like disgust. Suddenly I felt dirty, but it was too late. The doorbell rang again.

"I'm just going out. I'll be back early," I said. She was too stunned to even answer.

"Okay, so I'll just see you later," I said, filling in the awkward silence. I ran for the door, not bothering to let Ruben come inside.

The party was a college cliché—alcohol, music, trash everywhere. We began drinking as soon as we got there, and before I knew it, we were making out on the stairs.

"My grandma said to never go to a motel with a man. That's how you get pregnant," I said to him between kisses.

We never went to a motel, but after six months of dating I got pregnant anyway.

• • •

I sat on the edge of the bed staring at my reflection in the long mirror on my closet door. My makeup was done, my hair pinned up, and my frothy white veil pinned in place. I had been awake since five o'clock that morning, and now the house was filled with bridesmaids, hairdressers, relatives, and friends. I was in my room with the door shut.

It was just a month ago that my mom and dad had invited Ruben's parents over for dinner to discuss our future. "When she has the baby, they can live here," my dad said. "And we will help in any way we can," added Ruben's dad. I was twenty and had only been dating Ruben for six months, and yet it felt like a dream come true. My own family, my own life.

I excused myself from the table to get a glass of water from the kitchen. There, I found Grandma Fausta looking out the window. "Typical," I thought. "Eavesdropping again."

"What are you doing?" I asked. She quickly grabbed a rag and began wiping the counters, but she was sniffling and I knew that she had been crying.

"What's the matter?" I asked, looking at her tear-stained cheeks.

"You were supposed to be something," she said. "I imagined you would go to college and become a lawyer or a doctor. Now you will be just like your cousins in the Philippines. Young and pregnant with no good job."

She put down the rag and covered her face with both hands and began to sob. "What kind of life will you have now?" she asked through her tears.

And just like her words had stung me when I was a child, they did so again. I was supposed to be somebody, she said. It was ironic that the very moment she admitted that she had believed in me was the moment I failed her.

It was my wedding day and Grandma Patricia and Grandpa Paterno were on their way from Salinas. I hadn't seen them in months, nor had I spoken to them since they found out I was pregnant. As I stared at my reflection, all I could do was imagine their faces. It was almost too much to bear.

Just then my door opened and Grandma Patricia stood staring at me. She looked at me sitting there with my veil and began to cry. Grandpa Paterno came up behind her, walked through the door, and gave me a soft kiss on the cheek. "Neneng," he whispered. "You're not our baby anymore. You're going to be a wife."

Though I tried to fight them, my own tears began to fall. I had never felt such shame and sadness, because I knew that I had broken their hearts. I was the reason they had come to America, and now I was the reason for their disappointment.

"I'm sorry," I cried.

Grandpa Paterno gently stroked my hair. "You don't be sorry," he said. "You're going to have a baby; that's nothing to be sorry about."

But Grandma Patricia couldn't find words to say to me. The music that was in her when she first came to live with us was gone. She stood there crying until she reached into her black bag. "Here," she said, handing me a small white Bible. "You keep this with you and remember us."

As she headed toward the door, I thought those were her last words to me before I became a married woman, but then she turned around one final time. "Do not forget to cook dinner for your husband every night or he will beat you." And then she was gone.

After my son was born, all four grandparents decided it was time to go. They came to raise me and watch me grow, and now a new generation had emerged.

• • •

Maybe you will forget me. Maybe you won't remember how I cared for you and taught you how to cook and clean. I hope you will be good and don't forget. Your grandma is leaving you now. You have no grandma in America now.

Grandma Fausta, the first to arrive, was the last to leave, in 1991. She had spent a good portion of her life in America, but she said it was time to go home. Grandpa Sunday had left a few months earlier, eager to see the coconuts and rice being harvested on his land.

"You come Philippines and see me!" he said as my cousins and I all hugged him. He was holding his new Walkman and listening to George Strait croon to him through his earplugs. I was almost certain he didn't understand what good ol' George was singing about, but he was grinning ear to ear, just as he was when he'd arrived in San Francisco more than a decade earlier.

Before he left, my mom told him I was pregnant again. He reached out to me and in a soft, pleading voice said, "Do not have too many children. They break your heart."

That was the clearest English I had ever heard him speak, and before I could even ask him what he meant by it, it was time for him to leave.

Grandma Patricia and Grandpa Paterno left shortly afterward. As expected, Grandma Patricia wailed and moaned as we all said our good-byes. I stared at my mom as my sobbing grandmother hugged her, and I wondered how she felt and what she was thinking.

When Grandma Patricia let go of my mom, she looked over at me, offering her last words of advice: "Don't forget to cook dinner every night for your husband or he will beat you." Perhaps she had forgotten that those were her words of wisdom on my wedding day.

What happened between Grandma Patricia and my mom was never mentioned, except for one time, before I left for college.

"So what was the deal with you and Grandma Patricia anyway?" I asked my mom.

She sat on my bed and told me the story. I found myself listening to her the way I used to listen to Grandma Fausta, wondering if the things she was saying were real or fantasy. When she was done I sat there on the floor of my bedroom stunned. There I was, an average American kid getting ready for dorm life, in a hooded sweatshirt with the words "UC Davis" on the front, and my mom was telling me that my grandmother was hurting her through voodoo and strange magic.

If ever there was a Calgon moment, that was it.

Now it was Grandma Fausta's turn to leave and I found myself feeling strange, as if the last of my childhood memories were leaving with her. I sat next to her at the airport waiting for the final moment before she crossed the barriers only passengers could cross.

I remembered the day my parents and I went to pick her up. She was different now. She was no longer a stern woman with grandchildren to raise. America and the years had made her older, weaker, and kinder. And I was no longer the same child she met all those years ago. I was a grown woman, whose strange grandparents had shaped the adult I had become.

Yet Grandma Fausta was never one for emotion. She never told me that she loved me or that she was proud of me. The only sign that she approved of something was the deep dimple that formed on her right cheek when a smile would betray her poker face.

"I'll miss you, Grandma," I said, knowing it was almost time for her to go. It was the most emotional thing I had ever said to her.

She turned to give me a hug and began to weep. "Oh, Pati," she cried. "You were always a good girl." Then she tucked something soft and crumpled into my hand. I saw that it was the yellow embroidered handkerchief that she had used all those

Sundays she'd dragged me to church as a child.

I couldn't stop crying that night, clutching onto that piece of cloth she left me. I had spent all those years regretting the day she ever came into my life and questioning whether I really was as inadequate as she made me feel, and then in less than a minute her last words erased all the pain and insecurity I felt. All that was left was a frightening realization.

The Oracles were gone.

Chapter Eleven

Going Home

The blast of air from the vent above and the screaming baby kept me from sleeping.

I had a window seat on the cold 747, but there was nothing to look out at but the deep blue-black of empty space and the small ice crystals that were forming around the rims of the oval window. I had been on the packed flight for over three hours now. It would be another ten before our arrival.

I took out a pen and began drawing a dotted line on my napkin, tracing the flight's path from San Francisco International Airport. I didn't know where I was on the globe at that moment, only that I was suspended somewhere between America and the Philippines.

It had been twenty years since my last trip there, and I remembered hating it. I hated the unbearable heat and humidity, the pungent smells coming from the open market places, the merciless mosquitoes that sought after American blood, and the poverty that screamed out from all around me.

Look at her American clothes.

Look at her American hair.

I bet she won't eat that.

She thinks she's too good for us.

I could hear my cousins whispering to each other when I arrived. I was fifteen then. I could still understand my parents' native Filipino language, Ilocano, though I had some difficulty speaking it. I had the same skin color, the same eyes, the same

89

grandparents as they did, yet I was completely different. I was American, and their home was a strange, provincial land to me.

Perhaps it was the culture shock that prevented me from returning for another twenty years. Perhaps I wouldn't have returned at all had my mom not called me that afternoon. I had just started my new position as an editorial writer at the *San Francisco Chronicle*. All I could hear was sobbing on the other line.

"Mom?" I kept repeating. "What's wrong?" My father had passed away five years ago, and my brother and I were all she had. Worst-case scenarios were swirling through my head. "Tell me," I begged.

Finally, she gathered the words together: "We have to go home."

I had no idea then that "home" meant the Philippines. I left work early and rushed to the Financial District, where I found her small, frail body weeping against a cold concrete building. As she slowly told me what had happened, I knew I had no choice. It *was* time to go home.

I could already hear my grandmother's voice pulling me back to my childhood.

Your cousins in the Philippines are not like you.

They respect me, they do as I say. All my grandchildren there cook and clean. They work in the rice fields under the hot sun and then work in the house when the sun goes down. They do not know what it feels like to sit all day and watch television, or to go to the toy store and pick whatever they want. They only know how to work hard and respect old people.

You. You sit idle and complain if you are told to wash the dishes or mop the floor. You are already eight years old and you don't even know how to sew yet. You act as if you are too tired when someone tells you to clean your room. You do not know what tired means. Your cousins, they know. You're like sure.

My mom began coughing.

"Do you need water?" I asked. "No, but that air vent is too strong; it's giving me asthma," she said. "Why aren't you sleeping? It's going to be a long flight."

"I'm just thinking," I replied, staring at the dotted line on my napkin. "I hated Grandma when she came to America. She was awful."

"Shht! Don't say that!" she said, sitting up and shoving my shoulder. "That's the only way she knew how to raise children. You just weren't used to it."

"I guess she wasn't always bad. She used to tell me stories," I said. "While she was folding laundry or cleaning her room."

I always thought my grandmother hated me, but there were times when she read me the chapters of her life like a never-ending bedtime story. I would listen, wondering if the places and people she spoke about really existed or if it was all a fantasy.

"Tell me, Grandma," I'd say. "Tell me what happened next."

The flight attendant had just given my mom a cup of hot tea and she was closing her eyes as it made its way down her throat.

"Did you know that Grandma only came to America for you?" I asked.

My mother turned to me. "How do you know?"

I told her that Grandma Fausta would always end her stories with what brought her to America. "She told me you asked her to come take care of us. She didn't want to, but she did it for you."

I looked over at my mom and saw her well up with tears. "I know," she said, turning forward in her seat and closing her eyes again. I knew this meant she didn't want to talk about it anymore.

The Incredibles was playing on the screen. I was too distracted to watch. I wondered if my grandparents would recognize me now that I was a grown woman. They had only known me as a child, one who needed to learn discipline and respect.

"They'll be happy to see you," my mom said. "Especially now. They need all of us now."

But it had been fifteen years since they had left America to go back to the Philippines, and I had only spoken to them several times over the phone. I wondered what bond would be left between us, if any. And I wondered if all four of them had been carrying the same memories that I had been carrying since they left.

Especially Grandpa Paterno, who I had the softest spot in my heart for.

I had been on the plane trying to remember conversations I had had with Grandpa Paterno when I realized that there weren't many to remember. "Grandpa Paterno didn't talk much, did he?" I asked my mom.

"No, he was very quiet and very kind," she said. "Unlike..."

I knew what she was going to say, even though she stopped herself. "Yes, I know," I said. "I was there."

"Anyway, he didn't talk much, but you would always ask him so many questions. Even then, you were a reporter," she said. "Where were you born? How did you meet Grandma? What was your house like? You wouldn't be quiet, so he had no choice but to answer you," she said.

The credits for *The Incredibles* began to roll. I sat back and thought about Grandpa Paterno, remembering the calm he brought to my life after Grandma Fausta's chaos. I turned my head toward the window so my mom wouldn't see the tears forming in my eyes.

Grandpa Paterno was always my security blanket as a child, the one who loved and accepted me no matter what I did. And I let him go back to the Philippines without even writing or calling all these years. What would I say to him? I wondered. How would he forgive me?

I stood in the long line for the bathroom, feeling the blood rush back through my legs and feet. I had forgotten how much I'd hated the long flight to the Philippines the first time. Now I was older and it wasn't boredom but an aching body that was bothering me. I wondered how Grandma Fausta, who was impatient about everything, had endured the trips home when she would go back for vacations. She never looked happier than when she was packing her bags and preparing for the long flight. "I'm going home," she would say over and over again.

But I didn't feel that excitement on this flight. I was nervous about what we'd find when we got there, how I would act, and what I would say. My grandparents were strangers to me now, childhood memories that didn't fit in with my adult life.

"Maybe you will forget us when we are gone," I remember Grandma Fausta saying to me when she left America. But I never forgot.

Now I couldn't help but imagine her taking this same flight home. As a child, I would only see her walking away, waving good-bye and getting on the plane. "She'll arrive in the Philippines tomorrow," my dad would tell me. I couldn't imagine someone being in the air for that long.

"How can you stand it?" I'd ask her.

"Well, I have to go. I miss your grandpa," she answered. "And he misses me too."

My mom began crying again. I had run out of things to say, other than "It will be okay; don't worry."

"But what will happen now?" she asked, as if I had an answer.

"We'll see when we get there," I said. "It will be okay."

I worried about my mom when she got like this. She had inherited her father's high blood pressure, weak heart, and worrisome nature that just exacerbated everything. Luckily, she had also inherited his determination. I knew if I told her things would be okay, she would start thinking of ways to make it true.

Only I wasn't sure that everything would be okay at all, I only knew that the Oracles needed us.

"Drink some more tea," I said, looking for the flight attendant. In our family, tea was the answer to everything.

Turbulence woke me from the only nap I had taken so far.

My mom's seat was empty so I stretched my arms, hearing every bone in my body crack. I had no idea how much time had lapsed or how much longer it would be before we landed at the

Benigno Aquino International Airport.

I pictured our relatives waiting in the terminal for us with their ashy feet tucked into their flip-flops, and looks of hope in their eyes. During my first trip, they'd reached out to me, as if they were touching America itself. I remembered flinching, frightened by their unusual curiosity.

I wondered if it would be the same when we arrived this time or if their looks of hope would be replaced by sadness and uncertainty.

Maybe seeing the Oracles again will make everything okay for my mom, I thought. Except for one grandparent. Even though it had been fifteen years, I knew my mom wasn't ready to face her yet.

There were times my mom and I would sit alone together when the silence was filled with so many things I longed to say but couldn't. Here, on this twelve-hour flight to a land that was foreign and mysterious to me, I ached to reach out to her. But there was no way to move forward when the past still haunted her.

We didn't talk about it once during the plane ride, but I was almost certain my mom was thinking about Grandma Patricia. It wouldn't be right if we didn't visit her, but I didn't know how my mom felt about it, and I didn't want to ask.

Three hours left on the flight. My mom and I had gone the past two hours in silence. The closer we got to the Philippines, the more solemn we became.

I remembered Grandma Patricia telling me her final flight home was much the same way. She had called the house once she arrived in the Philippines to let us know she was okay. She was glad to go back, she said, because she missed her homeland, but she was sad because she would never see the Golden Gate Bridge or houses with wall-to-wall carpet anymore. God, she's so strange, I thought.

I pictured her on the plane, clutching her miniature Santo Niño in one hand and a rosary in the other. I could imagine the other passengers staring at her through the corners of their eyes, thinking she was a crazy woman as she spoke in tongues to ward the evil airline spirits away.

Grandma Patricia was always making a big deal out of things. When she and Grandpa Paterno moved to Salinas and only saw Grandma Fausta and Grandpa Sunday on holidays and special occasions, she would greet them in her typical style.

"Abalayan," Grandma Fausta would say as they hugged. "*Kumusta ka?* How are you?"

"We are surviving, with God's mercy," she would answer. I would always wonder why she couldn't just say she was fine.

"She's so dramatic," I'd whisper to my brother.

"She's just *different*," he'd say.

They were all different, especially from each other. But when I asked each of them why they had decided to leave America, they all had the same response: "I don't want to die in America."

• • •

"Too bad the kids couldn't come," my mom said. My son Robby was in his last year of middle school and Julie had just started.

"Please, Mom," Robby had pleaded. "I want to see the Philippines." But I didn't want to take them out of school, and their dad thought Mindanao was too dangerous for them to visit.

By then, Ruben and I were no longer together, but none of the Oracles knew. I sat on the plane remembering how disappointed they were when they found out I was pregnant, how they each looked at me with shame. The last time we were all together was on my wedding day. That was the beginning of my adult life and the end of their American one.

I looked out the window at the rich green and brown outline of the archipelago below. The thought of walking on land was inviting, but my heart was racing and my palms were sweating. From Manila we would still have to take a connecting flight

to General Santos City on the island of Mindanao, where my
mom was from, and then it would be another hour by car to our
destination.

The trip made me nervous. I had read many news articles on
the growing violence in Mindanao due to Muslim insurgents.
Several Americans had been kidnapped and killed. Just days
before we left for the Philippines, a local journalist had been
shot to death for speaking out against corruption among local
politicians. And not long before that, I had even written a col-
umn for the *San Francisco Chronicle* about the decades-old clash
between Muslims and Christians there.

As long as we didn't look "too American" we would be fine,
my mom told me. That was easy. My skin was the deep, muddy
sienna of Philippine soil, my eyes the shape and color of the
burnt coconut shells that lined the country roads, my hair a
mass of squid ink, a delicacy on the islands. Only I would know
that, inside, I was American.

Hot, humid air slapped my face as I stepped onto the tarmac,
as if to serve as a brutal reminder that it had been too long since
my last visit.

As we waited for our connecting flight, my mom briefed me
on what I should say when we got there, what signs of respect
I should offer, when to be quiet and when to talk. She began
repeating herself and fidgeting. I noticed her neck had turned a
deep red and the color was making its way to her face. She grew
agitated and broke out into hives.

I knew it wasn't my behavior that she was really worried
about—it was hers.

The small plane landed an hour later at General Santos, which
locals called "GenSan." The airport was so small there were
no terminals and only one plane landed there a day. Passengers
had to wait in a suffocating holding area while a team of young
local men wearing numbered orange T-shirts manually carried
suitcases and heavy boxes from the plane one by one. The men's
only wages came in tips. "Please, ma'am," said one to my mom,

pointing at his shirt. "Remember my number when you come back and look for me." Even in the stifling heat, their poverty prevented them from seeking any rest.

I looked over at a huge mural on the wall with the words "GenSan…WOW!" surrounded by colorful images of smiling children and adults carrying bountiful baskets of fish, bags of rice, and massive bouquets of flowers. The mural was not spectacular; it could have been one of many seen under an overpass in Oakland or Richmond in the Bay Area. But here, with these laboring men drenched in sweat and swathed in tattered shirts, I found the images of prosperity in the backdrop sad and ironic.

When all of our bags were finally recovered we walked outside, where masses of people were lined up behind an iron gate to claim their passengers. Some came merely to beg for money from the new visitors, many of whom they knew originated in America.

My mom and I scanned the crowd, looking for a familiar face. I spotted an old man, so thin I could trace the outline of the bones in his lower leg. He had a large canvas bag slung around his neck that hung down in front of his stomach. In it were small sacks of dried local fruit, garlic peanuts, boxes of mango and papaya juices, and small packages of snacks. The bag seemed like it weighed more than he did, and he looked over at me with pleading eyes and a toothless smile. "Snacks, miss?" he murmured. I shook my head and looked down.

We were walking through the crowd when someone reached out and touched my mom's arm. She looked at the man who had a head full of gray hair and skin like burnt leather before she realized it was her baby brother, Renato. She fell into his arms as they both burst into tears.

I had hoped my days of tearful airport greetings and goodbyes had ended the minute the last Oracle boarded the plane from San Francisco, but like everything else in this trip, it was time to relive and face the past.

As he and my mom cried, I placed a hand on my uncle in an effort to comfort him and to let him know that I was there, since he hadn't yet acknowledged me. They each wiped their tears and walked toward his waiting car at the curb. Neither of them said a word during the whole one-hour trip.

.   .   .

I remembered the Oracles as strange and compelling creatures who towered over me and who could change my mood from happiness to fear, sadness to elation, contentment to complete frustration with just one word or subtle facial expression. That was the power that each of them had over me.

But when I entered the doorway of the large home, I knew my memory had gone astray.

I saw a small, withered woman sitting in the corner of a long beige couch. She was surrounded by people fanning her and wiping her forehead. Her head was down and draped by a black lace shawl.

Her diminutive frame was that of a child's, but her hands were those of an elderly woman.

"*Ada dan,*" I heard someone whisper to her in Ilocano. "They're here."

The woman lifted her eyes slowly and locked her gaze with mine. I wanted to run and scream and hide. This couldn't be her, I thought. This woman is frail and weak and powerless. Her skin was like tattered crepe paper that had been crumpled up and spread out again. But her eyes were Grandma Fausta's.

She let out a long cry and began shaking. One of my cousins ran to get her water as the others frantically tried to calm her down.

I ran over to her, dropped to my knees, and laid my head on her lap. "Grandma," I cried. "Do you remember me? I am Pati."

But all I heard was her sobbing. "Grandma, do you remember me?" I pleaded. I couldn't control my tears. I felt shame and guilt and shock all at once. And all she could do was sob, tears falling from her cheeks onto mine.

Then I heard my mother's cries behind me.

I turned around and saw her in front of a shiny white casket trimmed with silver.

"Oh God, oh God," she cried. I stood up and put my arm around her, looking down at Grandpa Sunday with his hands folded neatly on his stomach and a black rosary woven between his fingers.

"Papang!" my mom wailed. "Papang!"

I looked down at my grandfather, whom I barely knew. Beneath the glass encasement, all I saw was a tired, small, old man in an American suit and tie. I longed to see him dancing with his Walkman, but I had waited too long.

"Oh, Grandpa," I cried, stroking the glass barrier. "I'm so sorry I never got to know you."

My mom and I stood there surrounded by all my cousins, aunts, uncles, and strangers, shedding our tears, begging for forgiveness, and realizing that Grandpa Sunday was gone.

"*Awanen ni lolo mo,*" Grandma Fausta cried over and over again. "Your grandpa is no more."

• • •

I opened my eyes and saw the green chiffon curtains swaying as the breeze from the rotating fan hit them. I was so disoriented I had almost forgotten where I was until I spotted a lizard crawling along the wall beside me. In the Philippines, lizards on walls were as common as ants at a picnic.

I didn't know how long I had been asleep, but the sounds of a guitar playing and people singing had woken me. I got up and slowly made my way to the bottom of the stairs, where I found myself trapped.

The house was packed. There was no room to move, or barely even breathe. Grandma Fausta was seated in a chair next to Grandpa's casket. Others were sitting on chairs, couches, and any vacant spot on the floor. I saw my cousins in the kitchen in an assembly line, preparing snacks and placing them on large platters to serve to the people. Outside the door, the sidewalks and streets in front of my grandma's house were filled with people just standing and facing the open doorway.

"Let us begin," said the priest who was now next to Grandpa Sunday. Everyone made the sign of the cross, and the Catholic Mass began.

I didn't know that there were no mortuaries in the Philippines and that it was tradition for the body to stay in the house until the day of the burial. I also didn't know that every night before the funeral there would be three religious services from three different denominations to offer prayers for my grandfather's soul.

After the hour-long Mass, I made my way into the kitchen to help my cousins. I grabbed a tray onto which they had placed all the Oreo cookies that my mom and aunt had brought from America. I had barely made it halfway through the living room before the platter was completely empty.

"It's from America!" I heard them saying as they grabbed handfuls of cookies and stuffed them into their pockets as if they were souvenirs.

It didn't feel right. My grandfather's casket was in the middle of the room and the crowd was lusting over Oreo cookies.

The next service was offered by born-again Christians and consisted of a lot of yelling and people saying "Hallelujah" after every statement the pastor made. In this case, they called her *pastora*. She was a short woman with a booming voice that kept asking the crowd if their souls were ready to face heaven or "heel." She went on asking the same question for two hours in the stifling heat while everyone was packed in the house like Philippine sardines. I thought I was already in "heel."

I looked over to Grandma Fausta, who was nodding off, but then she quickly jerked up again after the *pastora* screamed something into the microphone. Her unexpected cadences were like shock treatment.

In her best English, the woman screamed: "Prrray por da bereabed pamily ob Domingo!" (Pray for the bereaved family of Domingo.)

I pictured Grandpa Sunday laughing as he watched us being held hostage by the religious equivalent of an Amway demonstration.

By the time the final service ended, it was past midnight. Still, people stayed in the house and lingered in the nearby streets. It was like that every night for the next five nights leading to his burial. In fact, each night the crowd grew larger.

"You see how loved your grandpa was?" my mom said. "He was someone here in the Philippines."

Only then did I finally understand why he insisted on not dying in America.

· · ·

I hadn't had any time alone with Grandma Fausta. She was always surrounded by people I didn't know, in her room sleeping, or sitting next to Grandpa's casket, staring at him. But it was just as well. I didn't know what to say to her. Every time I came close to her, there was a vacant look on her face, as if she were in shock.

My mom and her sisters had been sleeping with Grandma in her room, sharing the bed that their father had slept in. Grandpa Sunday liked sleeping with a stiff board underneath his mattress to support his back, so Grandma had had her own twin bed brought in. Every night, after the services, I watched all of them retreat into the bedroom. I heard murmuring, gaps of silence, then murmuring again. I wondered what they were talking about and if Grandma was talking at all.

On the eve of Grandpa Sunday's funeral, I was sitting in front of the electric fan trying to find some relief from the heat when the door to the room cracked open. Grandma Fausta poked her head in and looked at me for a moment. I didn't know what to say. We hadn't been alone the whole time I had been there. She walked over to the bed and sat next to me, placing her hand on my arm.

"Are you doing okay, Grandma?" I asked, putting my arm around her. It felt strange, her hand on my arm, and mine on her shoulder. When I was a child, she rarely showed me any affection, and now grief and time had forced us into this awkward moment.

"I am okay," she whispered, her voice shaky and barely above a whisper.

"Why don't you come back to America with us?" I asked. "You can stay at my house." I heard the words come out of my mouth, but I couldn't believe I was saying them. This was the woman who had turned my childhood into a boot camp, and now the only thing I wanted was for her to come home with me.

"I can not," she answered. "Your Grandpa will be looking for me in this house." She began sobbing and soon I felt my own tears dropping onto my lap. We sat there holding each other and crying until she gently pulled away.

"I want you to be the one to give your grandpa's eulogy tonight," she said. "You will write it and you will say it in front of all the people," she said.

I was confused and shocked. Out of the forty-four grandchildren, why would I be the one to give our grandfather's eulogy? Of all the Oracles, I knew him the least. He never told me about his life. We never had a long conversation. What could I possibly say that would do justice to his ninety-eight years of life?

"Why me?" I asked.

"Well, you are a writer," she said. "And I know you have stories to tell."

She stood up from the bed and walked out the door. I had only a few hours to dig through my own memories of Grandpa Sunday and to remember the stories I had heard from Grandma and my mom.

Chapter Twelve

Discoveries

Grandpa Sunday had no nails.

When he first reached out to hug me, I was alarmed at the sight of his hands. He looked at my grandma, as if he wanted her to explain.

"Your grandpa has been working hard on farms all his life," she said. "He used to dig with his bare hands until he had no more nails left." It took a while for me to get used to it.

He would often use his nail-less fingers to scratch his head when he tried to talk to me. His English wasn't very good, and neither was my Ilocano. He'd point and say things like "You. How old now?" or "I'm happy. I'm America."

But he had a childlike quality and gentleness about him. I didn't need to understand what he was saying to know that he was a good man with a big heart.

I'd laugh, like I was watching my baby brother trying to form his first sentence. "It's okay, Grandpa," I'd say, rubbing his back. "We'll teach each other."

I often found in him the backyard carving wood, building tables and chairs.

He and Grandpa Paterno ran around like childhood buddies reunited. They would pat each other on the back, talking and laughing. They often took long walks and began planting various vegetables in the backyard. They loved each other as if they were brothers.

One day, their walk had led them to the nearest K-Mart,

which was nearly eight miles from our house. They came back carrying different bags and giggling. Grandpa Sunday brought his love for electronics to America and had purchased himself a new Walkman.

I was sitting at the kitchen table when he began climbing the stairs. He looked over at me and put his finger to his mouth. "Quiet," he whispered. I didn't know what he was up to, so I continued drinking my glass of Coke.

Suddenly I heard Grandma Fausta screeching, saying words I had never heard before. I ran upstairs and found my grandpa doubled over laughing. His Walkman was on the floor and the headset was on my grandma's ears. She was hitting him on the arm, furiously yelling out names.

By then, my parents and Grandpa Paterno had run to the room to see what was going on.

Grandma was too flustered to talk so my mom demanded an explanation from Grandpa Sunday, still laughing on the ground.

He tried to get the words out, saying that he went upstairs to show off his new "electronic" but found my grandma taking a nap. He slowly put the headset on her ears and turned up the music full blast.

"He wants to kill me!" she screamed. "He's trying to give me a heart attack!"

But Grandma found no sympathy in her audience. Everyone burst into laughter, telling Grandpa he was crazy, and telling Grandma he was just having fun.

I quickly discovered that Grandpa Sunday was full of surprises.

A few months later, he decided he was going to drive in America. He wanted to feel the freedom of the road like he did in Kiamba, with people waving to him as he drove by.

But when it came time for his driving test, he barely made it out of the DMV parking lot. In the Philippines, traffic rules and signs were merely optional. Proceed with caution, but anything goes.

So when Grandpa saw the stop sign as he was about to leave

the lot, he opted to ignore it.

After a short lecture, which he didn't understand a word of, the DMV instructor finally said: "No license for you. Come back in a year."

That, Grandpa understood.

Because there was a language barrier between us, Grandpa didn't try to spend too much time with me. He was ashamed that we couldn't have a conversation, and he would easily grow frustrated. "Poor Grandpa," I'd say. "Poor me," he'd respond, laughing.

· · ·

I think I was born on August 15, 1906, in the province of Pangasinan. A fire destroyed many of the townspeople's medical records, including my birth certificate. I was the fourth child of six, and the only son. My family was very poor, so I quit school after first grade so I could stay home and help my parents on the farm.

When I was seventeen, I left my family and moved to the town of Kiamba on the Philippine island of Mindanao. I was a settler. I heard they were giving away land, but it was dangerous. It was Muslim territory and they were very angry that people were moving in on their land. But I took a chance. I left my house with forty pesos, less than a dollar today, and one pair of pants.

When I first arrived, I earned money boxing. The matches would take place in barns or in cleared fields. I boxed until I earned just enough to start planting crops on my new land.

I started a business after I began growing and harvesting abaca, a plant that looked like banana leaves. The fibers were used to make rope. Then I began planting rice when I bought more land. I met your grandma when I started working on another farm for extra money.

I helped many people when I began making more money. I hired many workers around the town. I saved enough to buy a truck to transport the abaca and bags of rice into the city. I was the first person in Kiamba to have an automobile.

I was also the first person in town to own a stereo. I would invite
people from all over town to the farm. I would put the music so loud so
that everyone could enjoy the sounds. I was not educated but I loved
electronics and machines.

The more money I made, the more land I bought. You see, I had
no education, no money, but I went to this new place and became a
respected man. I worked with my hands and I worked hard. That is
how I earned respect.

• • •

My cousins were preparing sandwiches, coffee, and pastries
to serve the guests. This night would be the most attended,
save for the funeral itself. There was still an hour to go before
the service and already the two streets surrounding my grandparents' corner house were filled with people milling about.

There was a podium now set up next to my grandfather's casket, with chairs lined up in front of it. My brother had placed an
A's ball cap on top of Grandpa's casket, along with his Walkman
and a George Strait cassette tape inside.

I sat in the front row next to all my American cousins, each
of whom had prepared something short to say. We sat through
the service, looking at each other and then over to our grandmother, who was sitting in the chair closest to Grandpa.

"And now we will hear some words from one of Domingo's
grandchildren from America," said the priest.

I walked over to the podium and looked out at all the faces.
Outside the door, people were squeezing in, hoping to hear
words coming from America. I looked over at my grandfather,
still and silent, waiting for my words as well.

Good evening. I am Pati, one of forty-four grandchildren of Fausta
and Domingo Baigan.

It's been fifteen years since I've seen Grandpa Sunday, and I will
always regret that the only time I saw him again after he left America

was for his funeral. But as I look around, I am so grateful to know that he came home to a place where he was deeply loved. I see how many lives he touched, and I understand now why he always said he never wanted to die in America.

For many of you, America is a land filled with hope, prosperity, and promise. But it was never Grandpa Sunday's dream to go there. He had all of that, and more, right here in Mindanao, among all of you. He knew little English, but he had mastered five words: "I want to go home."

I couldn't understand why he wanted to go back now that he was in America. And only now I understand.

My grandfather was not an educated man. His English was poor and he was barely literate. Yet he died leaving each of his eleven children with land to call their own—land still bearing the fruits of his determination and fortitude. This land, his children, and we, his grandchildren—from Kiamba to California—are all his legacy.

He and I never spoke much. He would grow frustrated when he couldn't find the right English words to say. But as I look back, I realize now that I learned so much from him, not through his words but through his actions.

He often joked and teased our grandmother, even when she was in no mood. From that, I learned the importance of laughter.

I often saw him dancing alone with his headset on, listening to his newest cassette tape. He would take long walks with those headsets firmly planted on his large ears. From that, I learned to enjoy life.

Our grandfather was never lazy. If he wasn't taking a walk, he would be in the backyard building or planting something. Once I saw him making a large fishing net, even though we lived forty-five minutes from the ocean. "I like make things," he said to me. And from that, I learned how to be productive and make every minute count.

He often cried when he got homesick and thought of all the people he left behind in the Philippines—all of you here tonight. His old hands may have been rough from years of hard work, but his heart was as soft as a newborn baby. From that, I learned the importance of family and how to love.

We didn't speak much, but his time with me in America provided *me with life lessons that I've carried with me to this day.*

Grandma, I know you think I never listened, but I heard you. I heard all of you. Thanks for taking care of our grandpa, and for coming to America to raise me.

Chapter Thirteen

Rituals

My cousin Lani was handing us all black pins to place on our shirts. Everyone agreed to wear black and white to the funeral. The house was chaotic that morning. There were over thirty people in the house and only two bathrooms. There was no shower or hot water, only a pail placed under a spigot and a small bucket to use for pouring the chilly water over our bodies.

"Hurry!" my mom told all of us. "They're already closing the casket." My cousins and I rushed downstairs, uncertain of whether that would be the last time we would get to see our grandfather's face.

The pallbearers had already lifted the casket and were now walking toward the door. Suddenly, one of our uncles threw two live chickens under the coffin and our other uncle took out a sharp axe and slit their throats.

I let out a little yell, not knowing what was going on. All I could see was blood on the cement and the shocked bodies of the chickens still flapping their wings.

"It's a ritual," said Lani. "See the wings? They're bidding final farewell," she said.

They placed Grandpa's casket into a white hearse as we all piled into various cars. I heard a band with a trumpet and drums playing "Amazing Grace" as the caravan began to move. I looked out the window and saw a small marching band leading the pack. I looked to the sides and realized there were hundreds of people who had come to make the pilgrimage from my grandparents' house to the church, and later to the burial site.

The roads were packed, and I wondered if there was anyone in Mindanao, and even the surrounding towns, who hadn't come to say good-bye to my grandpa.

I looked out my window and saw a small boy holding his mother's hand. I felt a pang of guilt riding in the air-conditioned car. Behind us, all I could see was an endless stream of people walking with their heads bowed down.

The band was now playing taps and my mom was crying. "Who will take care of everything now that your grandpa is gone?" she asked.

When we got to the church, the pews were already filled and people were lined up along the steps. There were no windows, only open rectangles cut into the walls, and birds were flying in and out of the airy building.

I stared in awe at the crowd, trying to grasp just how prominent my grandfather was in this town and to these people. Dozens of our cousins did not even attend the funeral, as they were busy preparing the site for the wake.

Months before Grandpa Sunday passed away, he had begun building his own mausoleum. In it he built two tombs—one for him and the other for Grandma Fausta. The structure rivaled that of any belonging to a politician or similarly important figure in town.

Grandpa called the gravesite "my house," and he had built it along the border of one of his coconut groves. His children thought it would be best to have the wake there, and in one week they had managed to convert the area into a makeshift park.

Along with a team of my cousins, they had cut up large pieces of bamboo and made dozens of benches and tables throughout the grove. They created a "kitchen" by digging large holes in the ground into which they placed hot coals beneath large pots. To shield them from the heat while they were cooking, they strung together banana and palm leaves on top of a bamboo structure.

They had butchered three calves the evening before—just

enough to feed the hundreds of people after the funeral—and had stayed up all night cooking vats of beef *afritada* (stew), *pancit* (Filipino noodles), *lechon* (roasted whole pig), sliced beef with onions, and seaweed salad.

They had literally made enough for a village.

I looked across the aisle at the pew where my mom was now sitting with her brothers and sisters. My grandmother sat at the end where she was closest to Grandpa Sunday's casket. I remembered the fire that burned in her as she yelled at me to wipe the floors and hand-wash my clothes. Now, with her head bowed down and draped in black, not even the embers of that fire remained.

One by one, each family went up to have a picture taken by my grandfather's body. I found it strange and morbid, posing next to a corpse, but to them it was as if he were posing right alongside them. "Last picture with Grandpa," one of my cousins whispered. Only I preferred to think my last picture with him was at the San Francisco Airport, as he prepared to go home.

As usual, he'd had his earphones on and his Walkman blasting. He was wearing his green and yellow Oakland A's baseball cap, a red windbreaker, and jeans. "Last picture with Grandpa!" my aunt yelled as she pulled out her camera. We all gathered around him as he stretched his arms as far as he could, getting all of us under his wings. That was the last picture I'd remember of Grandpa Sunday, not this.

When the hour-long service was over, we stood from our pews and prepared to make the trip to the gravesite. My mom and I got into a different air-conditioned SUV, this time surrounded by even more people making the pilgrimage to my grandpa's burial. I wondered if we didn't need to slaughter more animals just to feed them all.

As the car slowed down, I could see plumes of smoke billowing above the coconut trees. I spotted my uncles and cousins, drenched in sweat and wearing tattered clothes. They looked more like hired help than sons and grandsons who were mourning the loss of their patriarch. They hadn't gotten to say good-bye when the casket was closed, nor had they even had a chance to break from their work as Grandpa's coffin was being lowered into the ground just a few yards away from where they were busily cooking.

"No!" screamed Auntie Minda, my mom's older sister, as the pallbearers began lowering the coffin. I looked up in shock to see her spring from her seat and throw herself onto the casket. "Papang!" she wailed. My heart began to pound; I wondered how long this would go on.

"Ssht!" my mom called to her. She walked over to my aunt and whispered in her ear, after which my aunt stifled her wail to a whimper and took her seat.

"There's always someone like that at every funeral," explained Lani.

"So, it's tradition?" I asked, utterly confused and still somewhat in shock.

"Yes," she answered. "Tradition."

Above Grandpa Sunday's coffin was something that looked like a heavy cement lid waiting to cover his site. Before the pallbearers prepared to move it, every person got a chance to walk by the coffin and say a final good-bye. Each of us broke off flowers from the throngs of bouquets and threw them gently into his grave.

"Bye, Grandpa," I whispered, crying more for the time I had wasted and lost while he was America than for his death in the Philippines. I had him there for all those years, and only now did I really know him.

• • •

I always found American wakes to be a strange ritual.

One moment everyone's crying and sorrowful, and the next everyone's eating finger foods and talking about Aunt So-and-So and the new car she bought. It seemed neither right nor natural.

But I guess it wasn't just an American dichotomy, for not long after my Aunt Minda had flung herself over her father's coffin she was laughing and smiling for pictures as she held a plate full of roasted pig and noodles.

My American cousins and I found a cleared grove where our uncles had set up a bamboo table just for us. There was a blue plastic awning to fend off the scorching sun. We sat picking at our food, looking around at all the people who were lined up to eat.

"Did all these people even know Grandpa, or are they just here for free food?" asked my brother. I had been thinking the same thing but felt it was far too cynical a comment to be said aloud given the nature of the event. Yet, not more than twenty minutes after the last person got his plate of food, the whole site was completely empty except for our immediate family. I couldn't believe that after the countless hours our relatives had spent cooking, not to mention preparing the site, all the guests just ate and ran.

"That's what they do here," my mom explained. "They think they're bothering the family if they stay, so they just pay their respects, eat, and go home." I didn't get it.

My eyes were swollen, my skin was burnt, and I was emotionally drained. By the time we got to Grandma's house, all I wanted to do was climb the stairs and lie down. I swung open the iron gate at the front entrance and prepared to do just that when an old woman came yelling out the front door. Shuni was an old hired hand and former teacher who had been around ever since my mom was in elementary school. She was the fortune-teller who had convinced my grandparents to send my mom to college in Manila. Now, however, most people in town just saw her as an eccentric whose life was guided by old wives' tales.

"*Gol-gol!* (Shampoo! Shampoo!)" she yelled, waving her arms, then pushing me toward a large basin filled with steaming, eye-watering liquid. She placed her hand behind my neck and pushed my head down toward the tub. I screamed, not knowing what she was trying to do.

She began to yell more as my cousins walked through the gate. "No one goes in the house until they dip their head in there!" she yelled in Ilocano. I looked to my cousin Lani, who had known the old woman since she was born.

"That's boiled vinegar," Lani said in a monotone, almost bored voice. "They believe when you come from a funeral that the spirit follows you, so you have to put your whole head in the hot vinegar to chase the spirits away."

My grandfather's body had lain in state in the middle of the living room for over a week, and just now this woman was worried about spirits inhabiting the house. I thought of the vinegar seeping into every orifice of my head, blinding my eyes and infecting my ears. Not only would the spirits be driven away, we would all be left blind and deaf. For a predominantly Catholic country, there seemed to be a few too many pagan rituals.

"It's the crazy lady, the crazy lady," my cousin Andrew mumbled to my brother. They both turned around and crept to the back of the house, where they entered through another door. I peeked in the front door and saw my brother smiling at me from inside as the old woman proceeded to push my head into the tub.

"Wait!" I yelled. I soaked my hands in the vinegar and dabbed my hair and face. She looked at me, deciding whether that was sufficient enough to ward the spirits away. I poured more liquid into my hands and continued to pickle myself. She let out a grunt and threw her hand in the air, motioning for me to enter the house.

Now, instead of going straight to bed, I had to run to the bathroom and pour cold water over my head to rid myself not of spirits but of the pungent vinegar smell that had penetrated my hair. I let out a little scream as the water hit my head, then reached for the bar of soap to lather my hair. I scrubbed so hard my scalp felt raw—and then I began to cry.

I sat on the cold cement bricks that lined the makeshift shower and sobbed with my hair still filled with soap. I wasn't crying for Grandpa Sunday or because of the vinegar in my hair. I wasn't sure why I was crying, but I knew it was time to go home soon, and at the same time, I felt I was leaving another home, one that I had just discovered.

Chapter Fourteen

Legacy

The night before we were to leave for home, my Filipino cousins decided to take my American cousins and I to "The Plaza." We didn't know what that was, but we thought it would be fun to get out of the house and not have to pray or recite the rosary.

My American cousins and I dressed up, wearing our best jeans, stylish wedge-heel sandals, and chic beaded tops. The guys decided to go commercial—sports jerseys, flashy Nike shoes, and other hip-hop wear. We each emerged from our rooms and headed downstairs to meet our Filipino cousins.

There they sat in the living room, staring at us as we descended. Each of them was wearing flip-flops, shorts, and a T-shirt. None of the girls was wearing make-up, whereas my American cousins and I had spent an hour looking for a voltage adapter so we could plug in our American hair dryers and curling irons. We had spent the next hour fighting over the small bamboo-lined mirror in our room so we could put on make-up that was now dripping down our sweaty faces.

Our American group stood there staring at our Filipino cousins while they stood staring back at us. It was like a scene from *The Outsiders*.

Finally, our oldest cousin motioned for the door and everyone proceeded to follow him. We had assumed "The Plaza" was located in an outlying area, perhaps General Santos or Davao, which were much bigger and busier than Kiamba. We stopped at the corner in front of Grandma's house, expecting a van or a series of taxis to pick us up, but our Filipino cousins continued to walk.

"Where are you going?" I yelled out.

"The Plaza," they answered in unison. So we followed.

Three blocks later, we came across a small park surrounded by vendors. The streets were lined with small open eateries and karaoke bars. The smell of barbecued chicken and pork was everywhere.

"The Plaza," said one of our cousins, spreading his arms out.

We walked into a place called "The Lechon (Roasted Pig) House," where we found two of our uncles already drunk off of San Miguel beer and their sorrows. "My family!" slurred our Uncle Bobot, the second to the youngest of my mother's siblings.

We took seats at their table, occupying most of the space in the bar. "We are the Baigan family!" yelled one of my cousins, to which all the other Filipino cousins cheered. My American cousins and I didn't know how to react; we never displayed such family pride in America. In fact, I spent most of my childhood years trying to denounce my grandparents and their names. Our eldest cousin ordered a round of beers.

"This is for Grandpa, and for all our cousins in America. Do not forget us," he said, lifting his bottle for a toast.

It took a while for everyone to clink their bottles together, and by the time everyone was done, many had begun to cry. They knew that in the morning we would be gone, to a land they had dreamed about all their lives.

And I knew that in the morning I would be leaving a place that was beginning to feel more like home to me than anywhere in America. This was where I really discovered my grandparents, the lives they led, and the land they left for me and my family.

I woke up the next day staring at my luggage. Outside the window a street peddler was making his early-morning rounds. *"Pan de sal!"* (Filipino rolls) he called out. *"Balut!"* (duck embryo eggs).

I slipped on my flip-flops and shorts, already dressing like a native. My cousins and I had stayed up the night before to prepare our things so we wouldn't have to rush in the morning. Now all we had to do was say good-bye.

Downstairs, our aunts and uncles had already prepared our breakfast: large over-easy eggs, *tocino* (red, sweetened pork), *longanisa* (sweet and spicy Filipino sausage), and fresh garlic fried rice.

I scanned the room for Grandma Fausta, but she wasn't there. Even after we had finished our breakfast, she was nowhere to be found.

She was holed up in her room, refusing to come out because she didn't want to say good-bye—not again.

"Let her go," my mom said. "She's too tired to cry." But I didn't want to leave without saying good-bye. I didn't know when I would be coming back, and the same thought kept haunting me: "What if she's not here when I do?" I didn't want to return only to bid her a final farewell.

I turned the doorknob to her room. Grandpa Sunday's twin bed was made, his A's baseball cap was sitting on his pillow. Behind the curtain was Grandma's bed, where I found her facing the wall, her back turned to me.

I sat by her feet and placed my hand on her leg. "We're going now, Grandma," I said. But she did not answer.

"Grandma, we're going now. I wish you could come back to America. I wish you could come live with me in my house." I began crying, wishing that I was a child again and missing the days when she would scold me.

I felt her shaking and looked up to see her crying as well. She began sobbing and wailing. "Maybe I will not be here anymore," she cried. "Maybe your grandpa will send for me."

"No," I answered. "You have to wait for us to come back next year. We'll be back to see you again."

Grandma sat up and put her arms around my neck. She was fragile, but she wasn't broken. "I will wait, if you promise to come back," she cried.

"I promise," I said, wishing that I could stay behind and shed my American life.

I handed her pictures of my two kids—parts of her legacy. She hadn't seen them since she'd left America, when they were still infants. She stared at my daughter's portrait. "You teach her to cook and clean," she said sternly. I let out a laugh and stood up from the bed. It was time to go.

Outside, my aunts were already preparing vegetables for lunch and dinner. The heap of long Chinese green beans were stacked on the round, plastic-covered table.

One by one, they snapped, providing a familiar rhythm that soothed my soul and saw me safely home.

Epilogue

The one-year anniversary of Grandpa Sunday's death was marked by a weeklong vigil and rosary recitals in the Philippines. My mom phoned to tell me it rained on the last day when they had prepared a large feast by Grandpa's gravesite. I had planned to go back with my mom and her sisters but decided instead to stay behind after I saw the cost of the fare. Work, money, mortgage—life wasn't so simple anymore. I still have time to keep my promise to Grandma Fausta, I thought.

"Grandma is fine. She's still strong," my mom said, with the sound of roosters crowing in the background. I pictured my grandmother sitting by Grandpa's large marble mausoleum, staring at the grave next to his, the one with her name on it. I could barely stand the thought.

I haven't spoken to Grandma Patricia and Grandpa Paterno in months, mostly because it was the same conversation every time I called. "I'm very weak," Grandma Patricia always said, in barely a whisper. "Your grandpa has to take care of me now. I will die soon. Will you come see me when I die?" I always laughed and told her she was being too dramatic. She had been claiming to be on her deathbed even when she was in America.

But as each year goes by, I know the Oracles are slowly fading. Though they left me and America years ago, the knowledge that they are still alive guides and comforts me. When Grandpa Sunday went, I realized it may not be much longer before the other three follow.

It was then that I decided to finish the story I had begun writing for my children—the story of my childhood with my grandparents. The kids were barely walking when the Oracles left America for good, and they would never know, or appreciate, the different cultures, beliefs, and traditions that their great-grandparents possessed, unless I told them. So I took out my laptop computer, scribbled memories on napkins and receipts as they came to me, went through old photo albums, and brought myself back to a time when I thought I was the most tortured little girl in the world.

While writing this book, however, something happened. The culture and generation gap I described would be nothing new to many immigrants, but to me, and American-born child, having all four of my grandparents in one household, blending and clashing their own beliefs with one another, was as strange and exotic as something I'd find in *National Geographic*. Our household was a sociological petri dish. What greater education could I have received about who I was and what my culture was about? Yes, they each wanted different things from me, often in opposition to my own wants and needs, but the differences between them resulted in the richness of my childhood.

I wrote this story so that my children would know a part of where they came from. But in the course of writing, it was I who discovered my roots.

Acknowledgments

Thanks to my children, Robby and Julie, for whom this story was told, and to Ruben for being with them while I was glued to the computer.

To my mom, Ludy, who spent countless hours answering questions about our family history.

To Heidi Swillinger, my friend, my biggest supporter, and my personal critic.

My thanks and praise to the people at Heyday Books, and to Lois and Gary for introducing me to them.

And, lastly, my deep gratitude to my grandparents—the Oracles.

About the Author

Pati Navalta Poblete is the deputy editorial page editor of the *Honolulu Advertiser*. Until recently, she was an editorial writer and columnist for the *San Francisco Chronicle*. She was also previously the paper's demographics editor, supervising a team of reporters who cover race relations, religion, gay and lesbian topics, immigration, and issues of youth and aging.

HEYDAY INSTITUTE

Since its founding in 1974, Heyday Books has occupied a unique niche in the publishing world, specializing in books that foster an understanding of the history, literature, art, environment, social issues, and culture of California and the West. We are a 501(c)(3) nonprofit organization based in Berkeley, California, serving a wide range of people and audiences.

We are grateful for the generous funding we've received for our publications and programs during the past year from foundations and more than 300 individual donors. Major supporters include: Anonymous; Anthony Andreas, Jr.; Audubon; Barnes & Noble bookstores; Bay Tree Fund; S.D. Bechtel, Jr., Foundation; Butler Koshland Fund; California Council for the Humanities; Candelaria Fund; Columbia Foundation; Colusa Indian Community Council; Federated Indians of Graton Rancheria; Wallace Alexander Gerbode Foundation; Richard & Rhoda Goldman Fund; Evelyn & Walter Haas, Jr., Fund; Walter & Elise Haas Fund; Hopland Band of Pomo Indians; James Irvine Foundation; George Frederick Jewett Foundation; LEF Foundation; Michael McCone; Middletown Rancheria Tribal Council; National Endowment for the Arts; National Park Service; Poets & Writers; Rim of the World Interpretive Association; River Rock Casino; Alan Rosenus; San Francisco Foundation; Sandy Cold Shapero; L. J. Skaggs and Mary C. Skaggs Foundation; Victorian Alliance; and the Harold & Alma White Memorial Fund.

Heyday Institute Board of Directors: Michael McCone (chair), Peter Dunckel, Karyn Flynn, Theresa Harlan, Leanne Hinton, Nancy Hom, Susan Ives, Marty Krasney, Guy Lampard, Lee Swenson, Jim Swinerton, Lynne Withey, Stan Yogi

For more information about Heyday Institute, our publications and programs, please visit our website at www.heydaybooks.com.

Related titles from Heyday Books

Perfume Dreams: Reflections on the Vietnamese Diaspora
By Andrew Lam

" Andrew Lam speaks to each of us quite individually and personally, with wit and compassion, about things that connect us all at the deepest level. *Perfume Dreams* is a fascinating and important book by a truly gifted writer."

—Robert Olen Butler, Pulitzer Prize-winning author of *A Good Scent from a Strange Mountain*

Trade Paper, ISBN: 978-1-59714-020-1, $14.95
160 pages (5.5 x 8.5) with 8 pages of b&w photos
Essays / Asian American

Farmworker's Daughter: Growing Up Mexican in America
By Rose Castillo Guilbault

"Rose Castillo Guilbault's touching and inspiring coming-of-age story offers valuable insights into difficulties common to Mexican children who navigate between two worlds. Writing talent sustained Rose Castillo Guilbault during her school years. It is this same talent that makes this work a joy to read."

—Francisco Jiménez, author of *The Circuit: Stories from the Life of a Migrant Child* and *Breaking Through*

Trade Paper, ISBN: 978-1-59714-034-8, $11.95
190 pages (5.5 x 8.5) with 8 pages of b&w photos
Memoir